American  Witch

American Witch

MAGICK FOR THE MODERN SEEKER

Anthony Paige

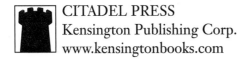

CITADEL PRESS
Kensington Publishing Corp.
www.kensingtonbooks.com

CITADEL PRESS BOOKS are published by

Kensington Publishing Corp.
850 Third Avenue
New York, NY 10022

All Kensington titles, imprints, and distributed lines are available at
special quantity discounts for bulk purchases for sales promotions, premi-
ums, fund-raising, educational, or institutional use. Special book excerpts
or customized printings can also be created to fit specific needs. For
details, write or phone the office of the Kensington special sales manager:
Kensington Publishing Corp., 850 Third Avenue, New York, NY 10022,
attn: Special Sales Department; phone 1-800-221-2647.

CITADEL PRESS and the Citadel logo are Reg. U.S. Pat. & TM Off.

First printing: December 2003

10 9 8 7 6 5 4 3 2 1

Printed in the United States of America

Library of Congress Control Number: 2003106185

ISBN 0-8065-2511-8

Contents

Acknowledgments   vii
Introduction   ix
1. The Witch: A Timeless Enigma   1
2. Wicca: The Origins of Faith   28
3. Wiccan Culture   71
4. Natural Currents: A Witch's World   98
5. The Magickal Basics   134
6. Spells, Incantations, and Invocations   170
Conclusion   209
Appendix: One Nation Under the Goddess   211

Acknowledgments

As always, Jane Dystel and Miriam Goderich were there every step of the way. Thank you for your guidance and support, and for providing me with an agency I can call home. You really are the best.

Bob Shuman, my editor at Kensington/Citadel Press (and reigning High Priest of Publishing), shaped this into a better book and helped me find the missing pieces. Thank you.

To copyeditor Kathy Antrim, for her eagle eye. And a shout-out to the staff at Kensington Publishing Corp.: Your hard work is greatly appreciated.

I extend my gratitude to Gerina Dunwich and Christopher Penczak, who so graciously agreed to answer my questions. (They write wonderful books and they're wonderful people, too.)

Thanks, M., for the nocturnal tour, and for spooking the hell out of me on St. Mark's Place. (Yes: I saw it.)

Kudos to Idanna, *strega bella*.

Throughout the writing of *American Witch*, I had the pleasure of meeting countless magickal people. Too many to name individually—you know who you are. Thank you for inviting me into your homes, your shops, and your lives. You continue to amaze and inspire.

Love and thanks to my very good friends: Amanda, Andrew, Jennifer D., and Jenny A. And to the SHPS crew, in honor of our reunion and those good old days back in the Bronx...Weren't we all just teenagers?

And to my nearest and dearest: My parents, for their constant encouragement (my mother for always pushing me in the right direction and my father for always asking questions). My brother, Joseph, is one of the best and smartest people I know, and my sister, Maria, is a powerhouse of art and knowledge. My aunt, Antoinette, shares with me a love of all things New Age, and what's more, she's always there to listen and encourage.

Till next time...

Introduction

This book is about the practice of Witchcraft in America. It also explores Wicca today—as a religion, a social movement and a metaphysical phenomenon. Who are the women and men readily identifying themselves as Witches? What do they believe in and practice? What are the spiritual principles that govern their lives? Such are the questions posed by curious minds, and they are answered in these pages. Inquiries of a more personal nature—specifically those having to do with rituals, spells and the concept of *magick*—are addressed as well, but they do not represent a definitive picture of Wicca today. What readers will quickly realize is that modern-day practitioners comprise a diverse population unencumbered by dogma and hierarchy, and so individual experiences and opinions do—and always will—vary. Unlike the majority of the world's dominant religions, autonomy is paramount to the practice of Witchcraft.

A number of recent books have attempted to compose a historical analysis of Wicca, but conclusive arguments are elusive. Many devotees believe that Wicca has its roots in Britain, where Gerald Gardner wrote *Witchcraft Today;* this now classic account of magick and ritual, published in 1954, granted the public an insider's view of what might have been a centuries-old coven. The book created a movement on both sides of the Atlantic and gave birth to what is now deemed the Gardnerian tradition. There are, however, other debates. The most popular shines a spotlight on the American folklorist Charles Godfrey Leland, who penned the equally intriguing *Aradia, Or the Gospel of the Witches* in 1889. Leland claimed to have found a surviving sect of Italian Witches who worshipped a Goddess, were skilled in herbal remedies and knew how to cast various spells. *Aradia* predates *Witchcraft Today* by more than half a century, but the academic threads attached to both are often too obscure to gauge. Interestingly enough, neither argument has hindered the resurgence of Wicca. Practitioners are not as concerned with the background details of their religion so much as they are with its future. Witches are real people. They know their deities and the system of magick. What matters to them is today, the proverbial here and now. And in America, Wicca is experiencing a colorful and vibrant renaissance. It did not begin in one specific place or with one specific person but is rather a fusion of the old and the new—that is, the old concept of earth-based spirituality and the new identity of the Witch.

Thus, *American Witch* is a primer for a new generation. While it explores the past—from the Salem Witch Trials to the rise of Spiritualism and beyond—it is centered on answering one question: Who is the American Witch? These pages reflect a large scope of research, and what I discovered through interviews and attendance at coven meetings and festivals was both enlightening and shocking. The American Witch is undoubtedly a unique identity made up of various traditions, beliefs and experiences. Men and women of all ages are following Wicca, but from a journalistic perspective, I sought out those who exist on the "fringes" of the movement. In the main, these are people who have discovered their spirituality through different—and sometimes opposing—avenues, honoring the Goddess and God but still clinging in one way or another to the religions with which they were raised. Others viewed themselves as Pagans and chose to combine the tenets of Wicca with darker aspects of the subculture. Initially, it seemed as though I was headed in any number of directions, but what I ultimately realized was that the term *American Witch* represents a mosaic of spiritual beliefs. Like the American spirit itself, the Wicca being practiced in America is made up of many backgrounds, cultures and creeds. It is not solely Gardnerian, nor is it rooted completely in the notion of lunar rituals and spells. People are reaching out and exploring a multitude of paths, and the New Age movement in America is a prime example of this numinous quest for understanding.

But *American Witch* does not end there. Along with the stories of many intriguing individuals is a practical handbook that includes spells, rituals and other metaphysical components. It is not a book of shadows, but you may choose to use it as a personal guide for better acquainting yourself with Wicca and the important role it is playing in society today. Practice is at the heart of *American Witch;* it is the most extensive section of the book because a Witch's knowledge is best expressed through magick and ritual.

As we will see in the following pages, a new generation is educating us on the varieties of religious and mystical experience. In doing so, they are redefining what it means to be young, smart and spiritual in America.

American Witch

Chapter One

The Witch: A Timeless Enigma

The man did not look like a Gothic Witch.

He was standing in the doorway of an old apartment building on Manhattan's Upper West Side. Dressed in jeans, a blue T-shirt and scuffed boots, he resembled most of the passers-by on this idle summer night. What distinguished him from everyone else was the snake draped across his shoulders. It was four feet long, thick and spangled with a shiny skin.

Even from a distance, I paused and reflected on the meeting that was about to take place. I had never met the man, but we had spoken twice via our cell phones and once online. A mutual acquaintance had brought us together. My college friend had been working in a pet shop a few blocks away when she became intrigued with an "unusual" customer. He bought mice and had asked her if the shop could custom-order a large glass tank. They struck up a conversation and she learned, rather inadvertently, that the guy was a Witch. But he didn't just practice Wicca. He "lived and worshipped" by night and enjoyed talking about "deity in the shadows." Obviously, my friend decided, he was someone I should meet.

Our conversations to date had been brief. The man's name

was Mark and he had moved to New York from Florida three years earlier. He was thirty-four years old. He worked the grave-yard shift for an investment firm on Wall Street, specializing in international client relations. Fluent in German and Spanish, Mark was a Gothic Witch.

I approached the doorway and introduced myself, though I couldn't muster the courage to extend my hand. "You'll have to do something with the snake," I said, taking a step back. "I'm not really a fan of reptiles."

Mark frowned. He cupped the snake's head gently with his right hand and turned its head toward me. "This is Fred," he said. "I know people aren't generally fond of snakes, but he's sort of my familiar."

"Well, I didn't come here to interview your familiar," I quipped. "But we can talk about Fred once he's put away."

Mark laughed. His blond hair was cut short, and the skin at his neck was peeling in the last remnants of a tan. He led me up two flights of stairs to his apartment and, once inside, carefully deposited Fred into a huge glass tank.

From the outset, there was nothing in Mark's apartment that looked particularly gothic. The walls were white and adorned with pictures. The living room was large, encompassing a couch, television unit, bookcases and desk. He had a fondness for Egyptian art, as evidenced by the small mummy statues gathered like an army on the coffee table.

I began by asking Mark to explain what made him a Witch, and what originally led him to Wicca.

"The basic answer is that I was displeased with my own Christian upbringing," he began. "It was fine while I was a kid, but as a teenager I fell out of sync with it. It was the whole con-cept of suffering and sin that I couldn't understand. To me, that wasn't religion. When you think about God—or in my case, the Goddess—you should be uplifted and happy. The smallest thought should bring you strength, you know? I didn't feel that way at all. What I *did* feel was a kinship with nature, but I didn't know that people were actually living their lives magickally, as Witches and Pagans, until I got to college in New Orleans and started getting involved with some of the local communities."

As a freshman at Tulane University, Mark found himself spending more time walking through the French Quarter streets than in the classroom. He met a Voodoo priestess who allowed him to witness a ceremony, and the experience moved him.

"That was my first look at the supernatural world," he explained. "I saw the dancing and the drumming, and the way people got lost in their deities, and a connection was made. It was beautiful. It was along the lines of what I had always believed—that spirituality should be celebrated. Voodoo is like that, but it has a lot of dark overtones that I identified with too."

Mark read up on Voodoo, Santeria and shamanism, but he felt a deeper affinity with the idea of the Witch.

"The Witch has always been a rebel," he said. "When you think of the Witch, you think of a person who can really do anything, who casts spells and prays to the moon and who can also brew tonics and heal others. The first Wiccan I met was a graduate student in New Orleans, and she totally lived her faith but she didn't wear it on her sleeve. She was a Witch, but the power for her was personal and it came during ritual. She didn't need to worship in front of a crowd or with a lot of different tools. That's what really brought me to the doorstep of Wicca. I was amazed by how diverse its practitioners were. I used to think my experience was uncommon, but the more I meet other Witches and Pagans, the more I realize how normal my path has been. I think that's an important part of Wicca in America—we're all searching for more meaning in the world surrounding us and not necessarily the world that follows."

Mark studied Wicca as a solitary throughout his mid-twenties. After college, he moved back home to Florida and tried to juggle daily life with his growing passion for New Age subjects. He attended workshops and festivals. He met with a number of local occult study groups. But something was missing. His interests in the dark phase of the moon and the lesser-known deities of the underworld had not found a comfortable outlet. He was practicing Wicca, yet he yearned for a deeper magickal experience.

"I've always had a predilection for dark things," Mark explained. "I don't mean the cliché stuff, like ghost stories and cemeteries. I mean the darker aspects of human nature and of the natural world. We're taught to fear everything that's dark, but I've always been drawn to it, and I've always thought that there was power in our own dark emotions because they take us to our true selves. I know it sounds convoluted, but think about grief and anger and depression. When we're in those states, we're truthful to our selves, and that eventually leads us to the right place. What I'm trying to say is that the dark is *transcendent*."

While still living in Florida, Mark began combining elements of shamanism into his practice. The altered states of consciousness took him, he said, to an "inner sanctum of the underworld." This was not, he quickly explained, a suburb of Hades but rather a shadowy counterpart of mysticism. What he felt was the power of balance and wholeness—of spiritual equilibrium. It was through the darkness, and through the invocation of darker deities like Hecate and Anubis, that he found great power and awakening. Eventually, Mark began calling himself a Gothic Witch because he felt the words best described his spiritual preferences. And his spiritual preferences have also become a lifestyle.

"I live completely as a Gothic Witch," he said. "To me, there's just as much power in a dark moon ritual as there is in a full moon ritual. When I call on the deities, it's always in the hours of darkness, and my psychic abilities are much more in tune with my magick. I still abide by the Wiccan Rede and the Wheel of the Year, but I think I differ slightly from most Witches out there."

In fact, Mark's views and opinions, as well as his brand of practice, are not unique. The darker aspects of Witchcraft—nocturnal worship, underworld Gods and Goddesses—are growing in popularity. Practitioners of this path meld traditional Wicca with Gothic undercurrents to heighten their spiritual preferences. In his fascinating book *Nocturnal Witchcraft: Magick After Dark*, noted occult author Konstantinos explores in depth those Witches and Pagans who feel the pull of the night in their magick.

Curious, I asked Mark to provide me with an example of the kind of rituals he performs.

"I'll show you one of my basic energy-raising rituals," he said. He then warned me that his magickal techniques were not common and would probably be a bit shocking. Depending on whom he asked, the techniques weren't even always deemed acceptable by the majority of Wiccan practitioners.

He cleared off his coffee table and then set upon it a tall black candle. In front of the candle he placed four smaller votives, two on one side, two on the other. It was a ritual crossroads. At the far end of the table he placed a black satin handkerchief that was folded at both ends. He sprinkled salt around the setup, then lit the candles and cut the lights.

The room took on an eerie quality. I watched as Mark closed his eyes and began meditating. His breathing, initially very heavy, slowed to a calm whistle several minutes later. His fists clenched and unclenched. The air was still, silent. I kept my eyes trained on the candle flames as they shot upright, then dipped toward Mark like a gesture of acknowledgment.

The energy in the room changed. Despite the heat, I felt a chill scale my spine.

Fred-the-Familiar was uncoiling in his tank in a far corner of the room. The thick, silvery midsection pressed and pulsed against the glass.

Mark opened his eyes slowly. He held out his right hand and motioned for me to touch him. "Gently," he said. "You'll feel it."

I pressed a fingertip to the center of his splayed palm. He was unusually warm, and it felt as though a drum were beating just beneath the skin.

"That's where my cone of energy begins," he explained. "I've channeled it into my extremities, and now I'm going to release it as an offering to the Gods."

"Why?" I asked him quickly.

"This is my way of paying Them reverence," he replied. "I've drawn this energy from the earth through invocation, and now I'm going to return it to the earth. If I were casting a spell, I would hold it for a bit longer and then let my goal manifest through it." Mark reached for the black handkerchief and unfolded it. Inside was a razor; the thin little blade caught the glint of candlelight. In one clean and fluid motion, he swiped it across his palm. Blood welled to the surface of the cut and ran down the length of his wrist before dripping over the votives, two of which blinked out. The tall black candle continued burning; its flame pierced the air and illuminated the circle between us. Mark held out his bloodied hand and positioned it directly over the heat.

I watched, speechless, as crimson dripped into orange and blue.

"I'm not feeling any pain right now because I'm in control of it with my mind and the energy I've just raised," he explained. Shockingly enough, he flattened his hand so that the flame bit into the cut. He didn't flinch. His eyes were trained on the makeshift crossroads, unblinking. "Anyone would look at this little ritual and see it as dark, maybe even scary, but this is my way of worshipping, and the dark Gods have given me the ability to take my spirituality to a deeper level. I have no fear of the razor blade, or of the blood or the pain. I'm way beyond that. My energy has superseded all of it and brought me to a new place. And to me, that's what being a Witch is all about."

"Pushing the boundaries?" I asked him.

He nodded and drew his hand away from the flame. He patted

the handkerchief to the wound. "Pushing the boundaries *fear-lessly* through meditation and ritual," he said. "I know plenty of Witches and Pagans who would disagree with me here, but the core of what I'm saying is true for every one of us. If you're drawn to Witchcraft, you're responding to an inner need, a desire to experience the esoteric and the mysterious. In the end, it isn't about being a high priest or a Gothic Witch. It's about connecting with the deities that will bring you to a heightened spiritual state, be it light or dark."

Demons: Witchcraft in Early America

It did not begin in Salem Village. It began in Windsor, Connecticut, in 1647, with a woman named Alse Young. Though she is acknowledged as the first person hanged for witchcraft in New England, little is known of her plight. There are no documents that effectively describe her or her accusers. We can imagine the humiliation and pain she must have endured, but public outcry was likely minimal. She was, quite simply, implicated and killed. The lack of records in Alse Young's case supports a sad theory: the local townspeople were so frightened by the thought of a Witch having lived among them, they wanted no future reminders or notoriety. Evidence of her mere existence and subsequent demise can be found in the diaries of two men—John Winthrop and Matthew Grant—each of whom wrote a few sparse words attesting to the execution. Alse Young the woman, the citizen, the human being, is lost forever. We will never know her last words.

In 1648, the residents of Charlestown, Massachusetts, chose their first victim. Margaret Jones was a midwife and healer and, according to local legend, something of a soothsayer. When those under her care grew ill or despondent, she was accused of

Witchcraft because of a "malignant touch." Her execution took place in June 1648. The terror even frightened the state governor, who allegedly spoke out against Margaret, claiming to have seen a "tempest" that tore down trees at the hour of her death.

In the 1650s, Fairfield, Connecticut, came under the Witch's spell. Goody Knapp was, by all accounts, a woman of high moral standard and favor. A devout Christian, she did not fit the mold of suspicion but was nonetheless accused of union with the devil. Goody was badgered to name other Witches, yet she resisted and maintained her innocence until the very day she was hanged. The town's founder, Roger Ludlow, created an even greater scandal when he claimed to have heard Goody implicate another resident, Mary Staples, for Witchcraft. Mary denied the charge and was never officially indicted. Here, we see the beginnings of that greedy circle, in which neighbor turned against neighbor and the hunt for more scandal escalated. One Witch was not enough.

A shocking case is that of Eunice Cole, who lived in Hampton, New Hampshire, and was accused of Witchcraft for the first time in 1656. Her sentence resulted in imprisonment and flogging. It was believed she had cursed a farmer's cattle. Though little is known about Eunice, records indicate that the Witch stigma followed her throughout her life. Even after her release from prison, people claimed to witness her uncanny ability to change shape and form at will. She was tried for Witchcraft several times but always acquitted. She died alone, however, presumably indigent, and she was consigned to a shallow grave. As the story goes, townsfolk were so frightened by the possibility of Eunice's avenging spirit that they drove a stake through her corpse.

Hartford, Connecticut, spawned a number of Witch scandals, but none so disturbing as that of Ann Cole. It happened in 1662 when Ann, a devout Christian woman, began suffering extreme fits and uncontrollable episodes of bizarre behavior. Her tongue became "possessed," and she reportedly spoke about people and events of which she knew nothing. Though she lapsed into gibberish, Ann often assumed perfect foreign accents. The height of her possession came when she accused a woman named Greensmith of evil doings. Greensmith was already in jail for suspicion of Witchcraft, but this did not stop Ann's fervent claims that something sinister was about to happen. Ann transcribed her visions and torments into a written account that was later presented to Greensmith. Shockingly enough, Greensmith was so astounded by the depth and breadth of the writings that she readily confessed to Witchcraft. The story does not end there. Greensmith's own tale of demonic enchantment bespoke of sex with the devil and secret meetings that were to lead to the signing of a pact. Greensmith was promptly convicted and executed. It is believed that Ann Cole recovered from her mysterious possession and resumed her stature in the community as a devout Christian.

In either 1657 or 1658, Elizabeth Blanchard Garlick, a resident of East Hampton, Long Island, was accused of Witchcraft when the daughter of a prominent citizen died in a state of madness. Sixteen-year-old Elizabeth Howell fell ill, and in her delirium claimed to see a phantom presence at the foot of her bed. She later named Blanchard Garlick as the source of her illness. Blanchard Garlick was apparently a middle-aged woman at the time, but that did not stop the local magistrates from assuming the motions of a trial. According to East Hampton records, over a dozen depositions were taken. The evidence, mostly hearsay, sparked a scandal that pitted neighbor against neighbor and raised fears of demonic possession. What is interesting about this case is that the accused was found not guilty by a jury of her peers. Elizabeth Blanchard Garlick was spared execution due to a lack of sufficient evidence—a rarity when one considers the scope of early American Witchcraft trials.

The Puritans sought God by all possible means. They adhered to strict social codes and highly structured lives. And yet, when they stepped away from their Bibles and scriptures, they saw nothing but the devil. Careful examination of Puritan life exposes this proclivity for damnation at every turn. When misfortune struck, the devil was blamed. When the devil was blamed, a Witch stood accused. It was a vicious cycle.

Salem: A Short History

The devil came to me, and bid me serve him.

   The madness began before Tituba spoke these words to her accusers, but her confession fueled an already simmering scandal. Had Satan truly besieged this God-fearing town? Which souls had he tempted and ensnared? Suspicions were churning in Salem Village in the winter of 1692, and Tituba, a slave from Barbados working in the Reverend Parris's home, had unleashed a poisonous floodgate.

   She was the third to be interrogated. She looked into the eyes of her accusers and admitted to a most disturbing sin. As the story goes, Tituba claimed a man had approached her and pressured her to sign a book in her own blood. This was to pay him allegiance. There were other signatures in the book, she said, but she could not make them out clearly. Her assertion added to the hysteria, for whom else in Salem Village had the mysterious man visited? The Witch-hunt was on and Puritan tempers were flaring.

   Tituba confessed to save her own life, but the enormity of the scandal had surely taken her by surprise. She could never have imagined that the simple games she'd played with the Reverend Parris's daughter, Betty, and niece, Abigail Williams, would ignite a maelstrom of violence. Tituba entertained the girls throughout the cold winter months with tales of her native culture, many of them rooted in Caribbean lore and Voodoo. She taught them palmistry and what today would be considered a form of divination—by dropping egg whites into a glass of water, the young girls were hoping to discern the identities of their future husbands. There was talk of the spiritual realm, of magic and the supernatural. The Puritans, of course, condemned such practices. Anything that bordered on diversion was considered sinful and dangerous, and the most innocent pastime could easily be interpreted as morally corrupt.

It is easy to understand the sense of enchantment Tituba conveyed. Puritan life, here, was a dark and narrow shell, devoid of recreation or entertainment. This was especially true for girls. Boys filled the otherwise lonesome hours with carpentry and fishing, but there was virtually no stimulating outlet for young women of the day. They were relegated to duties of the home. They breathed prayer and the scripture. In Tituba, they found something of an escape from the ongoing, dreary cycle that was made up of church and chores. She was a mysterious figure, perhaps even a rebellious one, for in claiming firsthand knowledge of the occult, she knowingly crossed the line into unholy territory. Tituba, however, did not instigate defiance, nor did she foresee harm in the games she initiated. In fact, several other young girls were drawn to the Parris home in hopes of joining the fun. They included Mercy Lewis, Ann Putnam, Elizabeth Hubbard, Mary Walcott, Elizabeth Booth, Susannah Sheldon, Mary Warren and Sarah Churchill. What began as mere amusement quickly escalated into fear when one of the girls saw a shape that resembled a coffin in a glass of water. Construed as a symbol of death, panic set in.

In January 1692, nine-year-old Betty Parris began having fits. Her body contorted. She screamed and writhed and made bizarre noises. The odd symptoms were soon apparent in the other girls as well. Alarmed, the Reverend Parris called in the village physician, Dr. William Griggs. Lacking a sufficient med-

ical explanation, he diagnosed the girls as having been be-
witched. The very mention of Witchcraft set Puritan minds
afire, as they believed irrefutably in sorcery and its capability to
cause illness and death. Here, a Witch was granted her power
from the devil. She did his bidding completely. The residents of
Salem Village gave credence to the more fantastical connotations of evil, wherein Witches flew across the night sky and animal familiars talked and tempted. There was no room for
rationality or the slightest bit of pragmatic consideration when it
came to religious affairs. The wisdom of the day was irrevocably
tied to the fundamentalist ideologies of the Puritan church, and
this enhanced their fanatical ways. Shortly after the scandal
erupted, the Reverend Parris said in one of his sermons: "The
devil hath been raised among us, and his rage is vehement and
terrible, and when he shall be silenced, the Lord only knows."

It was only a matter of time before the girls began making ac-
cusations. Tituba, Sarah Good and Sarah Osborne were the first
to be "cried out against." Each of the three women belonged on
the lowest rungs of the social ladder, a fact that undoubtedly
contributed to their swift arrests. Once before the magistrates,
both Good and Osborne firmly denounced any involvement
with Witchcraft. They did so in the presence of the afflicted
girls, all of whom reacted violently to the denials. The girls went
into convulsions, writhing and screaming out in pain, claiming
that the women's specters were roaming about the room. The
sheer intensity of the drama was overpowering, and it proved
too burdensome for Tituba. She fell apart under the pressure.
Hers was the first full-fledged confession. All three women were
eventually imprisoned in Boston, where Sarah Osborne died, reportedly in heavy shackles.

The frightening spectral evidence revealed by the ailing girls
was the source of further Witch-hunts. Soon, a woman named
Martha Corey was accused, much to the shock and consterna-
tion of the townspeople. Martha was, by all accounts, a devout

Christian and member of the congregation. Her fate, however, was sealed the moment she stepped before the magistrates and proclaimed her innocence. As they had earlier, the girls resorted to hysterics, and Martha was branded a Witch. She even drew suspicion from her husband, Giles Corey, who testified against her. The madness did not stop there. It expanded and found the frail, elderly Rebecca Nurse, long revered as an outstanding member of the churchgoing Salem Village community. Like the others, Rebecca defended herself. And like the others, she succumbed to the girls' performances and claims of torture. Perhaps the most shocking case of all those accused was that of Dorcas Good. A four-year-old child, Dorcas was deemed a Witch and imprisoned along with Marth Corey and Rebecca Nurse, her little wrists chained to a wall. Arrests continued throughout the next few months. By the end of May 1692, nearly one hundred women and men were awaiting trial.

The most notable citizens caught in the hysteria were John and Elizabeth Proctor, Giles Corey, Bridget Bishop and Abigail Hobbs. It is widely believed that Hobbs suffered from mental illness, but the Salem Village magistrates took into account her sordid tales of the devil and how her specter was used to torment the afflicted girls. As a result of Hobbs's claims, nine other people were arrested, including Mary Esty, a sister of Rebecca Nurse, and Bridget Bishop's stepson, Edward, and his wife, Sarah. Guilt by association was now a common thread running through the Witch-hunt delirium. When one fell prey to accusation, so too did his or her immediate family members. A sort of lineage had developed, and it began to seep out of Salem Village and into its neighboring communities, Topsfield and Andover most notably. It seemed there would be no end to the senseless arrests. The afflicted girls had become trusted founts of information, and the judges and magistrates relied on them to root out as many Witches as possible. They did just that, clinging firmly to their theatrics and enforcing the dubious assertion that specters be entered as evidence. Not surprisingly, the trials began in earnest.

Convictions were handed down swiftly, and Bridget Bishop became the first guilty Witch. She was hanged on June 10, 1692. Her body was consigned to a shallow grave on Gallows Hill, without the benefit of a Christian burial. On July 19 of the same year, Rebecca Nurse, Elizabeth Howe, Susannah Martin, Sarah Wilds and Sarah Good were executed. A most interesting footnote is found in the last words of Sarah Good; just before the final moment, the Reverend Noyes told her to confess to her sins of Witchcraft, but Good refused and branded him with a curse. She said, "I am no more a Witch than you are a wizard, and if you take away my life, God will give you blood to drink." Appropriately enough, Noyes died many years later, the result of an internal hemorrhage. He reportedly choked on his own blood. Giles Corey was pressed to death beneath stones on September 19. A painful fate, legend has it that Corey asked for more weight so that he might die quicker. On September 22, eight more accused Witches were hanged: Martha Corey, Mary Esty, Alice Parker, Margaret Scott, Ann Pudeater, Wilmot Redd, Samuel Wardwell and Mary Parker. Spectral evidence played a large part in the executions.

These marked the beginning of the end of the Witchcraft hysteria. No more deaths followed, but the afflicted girls had become celebrities in Salem Village and much of New England. They were even asked to help find other Witches in neighboring towns. Their reign, however, only lasted so long. With so many people accusing each other of Witchcraft, the numbers grew to impossible proportions.

What began as a sort of religious purging quickly escalated into a circus. The prisons were still packed, and the accused had to pay for their own stays. The disagreement over whether spectral evidence was admissible or not is what ultimately dissolved the Witchcraft court. After several months of dark hysteria, the judges and magistrates reconsidered the scope of the proceedings, despite the destruction that had already occurred. Such phantom proof was dismissed or, at the very least, disregarded.

The repercussions of the Witch trials lasted for quite some time. Families were ruined. Children remained without their parents and some of the most prosperous individuals were facing financial ruin. The general social climate was cold at best. In the ensuing years, people began questioning their actions and those of the magistrates. Had the devil truly walked among them? Had the accused and executed given their souls over to evil? Suspicion was cast on the afflicted girls, and rightfully so. Ann Putnam, one of the original children, went before the village in 1706 and begged forgiveness for her role in the tragic events. Was this in any way indicative of admitting her own guilt? Did Ann cry out against herself because she could no longer deal with the knowledge of her own possible false affliction?

We will never know.

And that is perhaps the most daunting aspect of the Salem Witch tragedy—our own uncertain theories. Hundreds of books have been written. Thousands of scholars have dissected the trial transcripts. New documentary specials are televised almost yearly, and each one attempts to illuminate another shadowy corner of the American Witchcraft enigma. No matter the scope of research, definitive answers will continue to elude us. But we can make one of two educated assumptions. The first is simply that the young girls honestly believed themselves possessed, that they gave credence to notions of the devil and his power over them. The games Tituba played might have impacted their already fearful minds. Fantasy and faraway terrors were twisted into reality. They were led amiss by delusions of Satan. The second possibility—and by far the most unthinkable—is that the girls feigned their symptoms, perhaps to escape punishment for having joined in on Tituba's forbidden occult games. Their own complicity would have surely attracted scorn. It is unimaginable that anyone could willingly and knowingly send innocent people to their deaths, but the probability of complete fabrication cannot be discounted. Let us not forget that as the scandal came to a close, the afflicted girls lost their credibility because they had simply gone too far. Even the most hard-edged supporters began questioning the violent fits and spectral sights. Another point that we cannot overlook is the basic factor of attention. These girls lived sullen, empty lives, and the onslaught of physical and emotional disturbances lent them an air of importance, if not outright celebrity. That demons were plaguing them had a similar, mysterious effect, for in what better way could they have warranted the concern of their God-fearing peers than to claim possession?

The Chronology of Deaths in Salem, 1692

June 10:	Bridget Bishop
July 19:	Sarah Good
	Elizabeth Howe
	Susannah Martin
	Rebecca Nurse
	Sarah Wildes
August 19:	George Burroughs
	Martha Carrier
	George Jacobs
	John Proctor
	John Willard
September 19:	Giles Cory
September 22:	Martha Cory
	Mary Easty
	Alice Parker
	Mary Parker
	Ann Pudeator
	Margaret Scott
	Wilmot Redd
	Samuel Wardwell

The Salem Witch Trials mark an important chapter in the ongoing story of the American Witch. She may have been eradicated through imprisonment and execution, but she did not die. Her legacy in Salem made a striking imprint on the fabric of our culture, our legal system and our history. She was an agent of change—and of warning. It happened once on American shores, but it would not happen ever again.

Salem Today: The Story of a Spell

On a recent visit to Salem, Massachusetts, I stopped at a small booth on Essex Street, where a pretty young woman sat before a table. She had flowing blond hair and wore simple jeans and a T-shirt. Peering closer, I saw the pentacle ring circling her middle finger. Jill was thirty-one, a wife, mother and Wiccan priestess. Three days a week, she took up a spot on Essex Street where, for thirty dollars, she would offer a complete psychic consultation. I took a seat opposite her and slid my money across the table. Before she reached for her deck of worn cards, I questioned her about the Wiccan philosophy on psychic abilities.

"It's very simple," she told me. "Witches believe that the human mind can transcend the five senses through regular meditation. You have to be willing to sort of think of the mind as a muscle: if you work it out, it'll get stronger. You don't have to be born with psychic ability; everyone has the potential to be psychic. It's a normal part of a Witch's daily life. The more a person gets in touch with the natural forces of the earth, the more heightened his awareness is."

"So," I said facetiously, "can you read my mind?"

She laughed. "No, I can't do that. But I can read your aura." Jill had come to the Wiccan religion in her early twenties. After earning a degree in history, she traveled extensively throughout the United States, where she came in contact with several Native American tribes. A Choctaw shaman taught her the method of "inner breathing," which calls for a person to inhale, hold that breath for five seconds, and then exhale nasally for a count of eight seconds. Done repeatedly, she said, one became relaxed and could therefore meditate easily. Later, the shaman instructed her to simply "order her mind to receive information." The breathing method and meditation served her well for several years, regulating her stress levels and even alleviating the pain of a childhood injury. Eventually, Jill began to see colors around people, faint traces of light that usually hovered just above a person's hairline. The uncanny ability strengthened with time. It wasn't something she could turn off at will. Other strange phenomena started occurring in her life shortly thereafter. Upon looking at a person, letters immediately popped into her head.

"It was the strangest thing," she said. "I would meet someone for the first time and suddenly a discombobulated alphabet would pop into my head. When I first met my sister's boyfriend, the letter *H* came into my mind. I asked him if he knew anyone of personal importance whose name began with that letter, and he perked right up. The day before, he'd visited with his stepbrother, Harold, and had been thinking of the guy ever since. It was odd, to say the least."

Confused about her newly discovered abilities, Jill, living in Maine at the time, began reading about the resurgence of Wicca in America and haunting a local New Age shop. The owner, she later discovered, was a Wiccan priest who ran a coven. Jill began studying what she called the "art and science of Witchcraft" and was then initiated by the shop's owner. When she was twenty-six, she attended a public "Witch-out" in Bangor to celebrate the winter solstice, and there met her husband. They moved to Salem one year later and decided against practicing in a coven. They were solitaries, casting spells or drawing down the moon in the privacy of their own bedroom.

Promptly, I asked Jill what she saw in my aura.

She stared at my head and squinted. "Actually, there's a lot of green in your aura, which tends to symbolize luck. I see a little blue, too, which usually means that a person has an overall calm demeanor."

"Can you see anything else?" I pressed, unsatisfied.

"Well, I can't see anything, but I'm getting images. They're like feelings, hunches. I get the sense that you're a very literate person because I feel you surrounded by books..."

My interest level instantly peaked, but I said nothing.

Jill continued to stare at me. "Are you a writer?"

Not bad, I thought. I nodded.

She looked pleased. "When it comes to your career, I get the letters *A* and *G* as being important, and the letters *P* and *J*. You're surrounded by the letter *J* a lot."

It did ring true, to some extent. Over the course of thirty minutes, Jill read my Tarot cards, palms and tea leaves. She keyed in on a few impressive facts without my assistance.

Even after my thirty-minute session surpassed the forty-minute mark, Jill and I remained immersed in conversation. I learned that, aside from practicing Wicca, she lived a relatively normal life. She taught adult education courses in nearby Boston. She volunteered at a local hospital. Her husband was a scientist and they were raising their daughter as a Witch. They had been married in a Wiccan handfasting ceremony, in which marital vows are pledged within the magick circle. In the main, Jill spent her free time meditating and gardening. She tended her flowers and vegetables by the phases of the moon. She told me she was an "active" Witch, often casting spells and performing rituals three or even four times per week. During the waning phase of the moon, she centered her energy on banishing negativity from her life. On the nights of the waxing moon she concentrated on healing rituals and prosperity. She owned no ritual robes, prefer ring instead to just work in comfortable clothing—jeans, T-shirts, shorts.

"I'm not all that theatrical a Witch," she confessed. "I don't equate my religion with appearance. It's a very personal thing. In a place like Salem, you see Witches running around in capes, and that's fine, but I'm a bit more conventional. I don't feel as if I need to prove anything. I'm strong in every aspect of my life as a Witch."

Jill's strongest aspect, she felt, was her spell-casting ability. She took great care in choosing the proper moon phases, herbs and candle colors to ensure the success of a particular spell. Like most Witches, she believed in astrology and the influence of planetary positions. A love spell, for example, would produce the best results if done in a waxing phase of the moon, utilizing a red candle, on a Friday night because Friday is sacred to the Goddess of love.

"It amazes me that people get so freaked out by the word *spell*," she said. "It really is a prayer. The candles, the herbs, the incense—they're just tools that help center energy. Real magick exists inside and outside of the mind. When a Witch casts a spell, she doesn't ask the Goddess to grant her a particular wish. As a Witch I invoke the Goddess from within, because the Goddess is already a part of me."

When I returned to Salem a few weeks later, I ran into Jill at a local restaurant, where we struck up our conversation as if no time had passed between us. We talked over coffee, and it wasn't long before she invited me to her home. There, I met her husband and daughter. It was a modest house, filled with family photographs and shelves of books. My inquisitiveness about her magickal side, Jill said, struck a chord in her, and she wanted to show me just how "normal" a life she lived. She led me through the rooms, pointing out the awards she had won for community service. Aside from the multitude of books about Wicca that were scattered everywhere, there was no indication of her identity as a Witch. Eventually we came upon a small pantry off the kitchen, no larger than a walk-in closet. A table was pushed against the wall. A single window faced the wooded yard and soaked up the moonlight. The floor was hardwood and stacked with boxes of candles, incense and oils. It was the private alcove where Jill and her husband practiced as solitaries.

"You see?" Jill remarked. "Simple. And it works like a charm. I think about eighty percent of Wicca today is born of sheer creativity. Solitary Witches and covens create their own rituals that call for different methods, different techniques. I think if a Witch's intention is pure and her energy focused, a white candle might work just as well as a red one where a love spell is concerned. Or any spell or ritual, for that matter."

Jill and I sat at the small table in her "magick room." The moon was waxing and in the astrological sign of Leo. It was a good time to cast spells for career, money, success. Eager to join a solitary Witch at work, I asked her if we could cast one together. "Sure," she answered cheerfully. "What would you like to cast a spell for?"

I thought about it for a moment. The answer didn't surprise me: "Money."

Jill laughed. "Fine. Let's do it together." She retrieved a thin green candle, no more than six inches in length, from the shoebox on the floor. Beside it on the table she placed a vial of myrrh-scented oil and a salt shaker filled with cinnamon. The important thing to remember when casting a spell, we both agreed, was that the end result—if one even evolved—didn't always show itself clearly. Jill had cast spells in the past that merely created certain situations through which her intended goal could be reached. I'd had similar experiences. Perhaps our conjoined energy would manifest a minor money miracle.

Jill began by taking my hands in hers and instructing me to

close my eyes, breathe deeply and clear my mind of extraneous thoughts. We concentrated on the droning silence. Eventually, I felt myself begin to relax. Halfway through, I opened my eyes and glanced at Jill. Her face was tilted upward, a calm smile gracing her lips. I held her hands and felt her pulse quicken. She was raising energy with precision. A feverish heat emanated from her palms. Moments later, she handed me the candle and I anointed it with the myrrh oil. Next, using a clean sewing needle, I inscribed my name into the stiff, slippery wax along with my date of birth. I drew a little dollar sign just beneath the wick. Jill performed the same steps. Finally, we sprinkled cinnamon over the candle. This was a common and widely used spell, and one known to produce results.

"Okay, let's go for it," Jill said. "Goddess and God, here we come."

I shut my eyes again and began visualizing. I simply pictured my frighteningly thin wallet growing thick with twenty-dollar bills, falling against each other like dominos. I inhaled the scent of cinnamon and myrrh and then placed the candle in its holder. Jill lit the wick. The flame jumped up. I looked at her and we joined hands again. We sat meditating in silence for several minutes. We had not cast a magick circle, nor had we recited any charge or verse. Our energy was strong and focused and we were both experienced enough to get through the spell without them.

Jill cupped her fingers around the dancing flame. She said: "In the name of the Great Goddess, I ask that this spell be done correctly and for the good of all." It was the end of our spell-casting session. I felt exhilarated yet oddly drained as I watched the green wax dribble onto the tabletop. Jill told me she would allow the candle to burn itself out completely and that we should not think about the spell in the coming days and weeks.

I did not think about it again until nearly a month later, when I came home from work and found an envelope waiting for me in the mailbox. It was a letter from a magazine to which I had submitted an essay several weeks earlier. They had accepted the essay for publication. Clipped to the letter was an agreement that stated my pay of a few hundred dollars. Stunned, I remembered the spell I had cast with Jill in Salem. We had projected for money, and it seemed half of our goal had been accomplished. A few days later, Jill phoned me to tell me that she had experienced a similar little boost in her finances. A local community center phoned her and asked if she'd be willing to conduct a workshop about Wicca. It was short notice, but the pay was more than fair. It was a thrilling feeling. We spent the remainder of our conversation discussing magickal techniques and planning further spells together.

The First Spirit: Native America

Native American spirituality and Wicca are not parallel religions, but they share a number of intriguing similarities. According to Native American lore, every object possesses its own distinct spirit, from the smallest rock to the tallest redwood tree. It has been said that the Native American "Bible" lives on the wind and cannot ever be torn, burned or disseminated. Theirs is a timeless history. And, like Wicca's, the Native American concept of spirituality is centered on Mother Earth and the sacredness of the natural world. The shifting patterns of the seasons mark powerful moments in the atmosphere for Witches and Native American shamans alike. There is also the significance of ritual in the faiths of both; the sun, moon and the elements are necessary when trying to harness any union with the divine.

Heather, a twenty-eight-year-old Arizona Native American, spent much of her youth living on and off reservations. Her fa-

LAURIE CABOT

The "Official Witch of Salem," Laurie Cabot was born in Oklahoma and lived much of her childhood in Anaheim, California. She relocated to Boston at fourteen. In her early years, she experienced a number of supernatural occurrences that led her to believe in her own psychic gifts. She also felt a powerful affinity with Witches. Cabot often claims that she is descended from a long line of Celtic Witches.

As a teenager, Cabot spent much time in her local library scouring books about religion. It was there that she befriended a woman who suggested a perusal of paranormal and occult-related titles. Later, the woman revealed herself to Cabot as a Witch and, in the process, introduced her to two other female Witches. According to Cabot, all three women initiated and schooled her in the ways of Witchcraft. Their lessons served her well. Cabot went on to open a successful shop, Crow Haven Corner, in Salem, which was followed by a second called The Cat, The Crow and The Crown; both are major tourist attractions. A successful businesswoman, Cabot is also the author of four best-selling books: *Power of the Witch, Celebrate the Earth, Love Magic* and *The Witch in Every Woman.* She founded the Cabot Tradition of the Science of Witchcraft and spent many years teaching her own interpretation of magick, ritual and Goddess worship.

Cabot has an international reputation as a spokesperson for the Pagan community. She always wears her Witch's robes in public and has long vowed to live her life "totally as a Witch." An activist, she founded the Witches League for Public Awareness (WLPA) in Salem, a nonprofit organization dedicated to negating misrepresentation of Witches and Wicca in the media. She lives, teaches and practices in Salem.

www.lauriecabot.com

ther was a full-blooded Cherokee. Her mother was one-quarter Lakota. Because her parents separated when she was eight, Heather grew up in a "traditional Christian home, but also in the shadow of Native American spirituality." She attended her first powwow at the tender age of eleven and later watched her father counsel the elders on his reservation. Today, Heather's spiritual identity is made up of Native American and Pagan beliefs.

"I wouldn't exactly label myself a Witch in the traditional sense," she explained. "I was never initiated to practice Wicca, but because I'm Native American, I understand what it means to live according to nature and the cycles. I know the magic and the possibilities that are alive in nature."

As a practitioner of eclectic spirituality, Heather combines elements of Wicca with those of Native American mysticism. The two, in her view, are closely linked.

"Traditionally, Native Americans perceived the earth as divine," she said. "There was a lot of lunar worship. Certain deities ruled the sun, others had precedence over the stars and the waters and skies. When I first read about Wicca, I wasn't at all surprised or confused by it. It made perfect sense to me. A lot of Native American spirituality has survived throughout the centuries, and I think it's helped the whole New Age movement immeasurably. Years ago, when people became entranced by crystals and stones, they looked back to Native American influences and saw that we viewed everything as sacred. Same thing with Witches and spells. Native Americans have been using the elements and their focused prayers in the same way for countless years. It's nothing new to us."

Heather studied comparative religion in college. Today, she believes that her Native American ancestors were the first true shamans and Witches in America. "Native American history is very rich in supernatural lore," she said. "There was always a concept of deity and of the Great Spirit. We know that Vision

Quests were a common practice when boys reached puberty;
they fasted for days and were then sent out into the wilderness to
wait for visions and signs from the Masters. The Sun Dances are
thought to reenact the creation story. Growing up, I knew about
Medicine Men who could heal you with their touch, or by mix-
ing certain herbs and roots together. That's the real stuff. That's
the magick that today's Witchcraft tries to emulate, but it was
alive here on the plains long before anyone even knew the word
Witch."

For Heather, divinity is about honoring the old while ushering in the new. Her Native American roots, coupled with her interests in Wicca, provide the perfect foundation for spiritual
growth.

"We know the Native Americans were here long before the
Salem Witch Trials, and they were still here during and after
them," she said. "When you think about the chronology of the
supernatural in America, you have no choice but explore Native
American spirituality. It didn't begin or end at one specific time,
and it will never disappear. In that sense, it's a lot like the concept of Witchcraft, which has also been around for as long as
time. It's all here to stay."

Sacred Site

GALLOWS HILL, SALEM, MASSACHUSETTS

The Witch Trials of 1692 occurred in what is now Danvers, Massachusetts. A short distance away is the picturesque town of Salem, where today's modern-day Witches dominate the population. Each year, on the eve of Samhain, countless individuals hold a candlelight vigil on Gallows Hill, the site of the infamous hangings. In doing so, they honor those who died and celebrate their own identities as Witches, Pagans and Goddess-worshippers. Gallows Hill may not look as it did three centuries ago, but the mystery and history have never quite left the air. It is a sacred site. Devotees of the Wiccan faith are reminded of their own religious freedom here because of the injustices the word *Witch* once incurred. But no American—regardless of religious preference—will leave Gallows Hill unmoved. A part of our nation's history, it sheds light on how people once lived and died, and of how society has progressed both intellectually and spiritually.

Chapter Two

Wicca: The Origins of Faith

It was the end of the nineteenth century and the beginning of the twentieth that saw an unexpected peak in notions of the afterlife. As society developed and religious beliefs moved further away from the extremes, large numbers of people began considering the possibility of an alternate reality—a *spirit* realm. Mediums, clairvoyants and channelers performed remarkable otherworldly feats that garnered praise from skeptics and curious minds alike. The dead, suddenly, did not seem so unreachable. This new era marked the birth of Spiritualism.

For the first time, odd or inexplicable occurrences were not immediately blamed on evil forces. There were no demons in the air, nor did the budding psychic find herself at the center of any potentially fatal scandals. Interest levels rose. Conservative theological restraints were loosening a bit at the seams. The Witch was still a taboo identity, but the foundation that would later support her resurgence had been laid down. In addition to communication with the dead, Spiritualism embraced radical concepts of healing and reincarnation. A popular practice was psychic diagnosis, in which a medium divined illness via his or her extrasensory abilities. Seances were equally prevalent. The Other Side wanted to speak, and people were listening.

In the United States, Spiritualism is commonly linked to the Fox sisters, who in 1848 began communicating with spirits through rapping, knocking and clapping. It all started in the small town of Hydesville, New York. Fourteen-year-old Maggie Fox and her eleven-year-old sister, Katie, heard bizarre banging noises in their home after nightfall. Their mother, Mrs. Fox, blamed the sounds on ghostly phenomena. The girls were curious and began studying the noises more closely. They discovered that a certain conversation had developed by way of their own hand clapping, as the raps seemed to respond to their questions. Eventually, the spirit identified himself as Charles Rosa and claimed to have been murdered by the former occupant of the house. Human remains were unearthed after digging commenced in the cellar. The Fox sisters created a press sensation and went on to shadow a large part of the publicity circuit, and although the sisters were later plagued by scandal and illness, they introduced America to a spookier side.

Modern-day Witchcraft has always embraced the supernatural realm. Indeed, the men and women who call themselves Witches view the unexplained as wholly natural, one of a thousand currents alive in the universe. The supernatural, here, does not relate solely to ghosts and the proverbial haunted house; it extends beyond these boundaries and includes psychic phenomena, clairvoyance, clairaudience, ESP, channeling, dowsing, divination and spirit communication. It was this way in ancient times as well. The village Witch practiced folk magick, and she also knew how to peer into the future, summon the winds and exorcise demons. Magick, though born in the mind, is also considered a part of the supernatural because its results are ultimately attained through unexplained means. A Witch harnesses the forces that with time and practice become very tangible, but the source of power is and will remain a beautiful mystery.

The old adage that a Witch "walks between the worlds" is rooted in the average person's perception of the atmosphere. He or she will go about daily life confined by five meager senses, content in the belief that nothing exists just out of sight. The majority of people adhere to this mode of thinking; they put credence in the concrete and dismiss what cannot be proven. They see the world in filtered shades, unaware that our surroundings truly are Technicolor. When people discover Wicca, they put aside these man-made laws and quickly come to understand nature as ripe with unseen forces. Through meditation and ritual, they chip away at the hard edges of skepticism, eventually opening the door to enchantment. As a mystery tradition, Wicca does not seek to define the supernatural. Wicca accepts the unexplained and builds upon its foundation.

Hawaii: Land of Magick, Land of Myth

Hawaii is a popular destination for all the right reasons: cobalt skies, ocean breezes, a mountainous terrain dotted by wildflowers. Tourists flock by the thousands to swim and frolic in the waters of the Pacific or to gaze up at the mottled rock formations born of lava and ash. Behind the breathtaking scenery, however, lies a history rich in myth, lore and magickal tradition.

Christian missionaries did not set foot on Hawaiian shores until 1820. Surely they were surprised to find much of this Polynesian culture intact, replete with a pantheon of Gods, Goddesses and demi-gods. Theirs was a complex system of belief rooted directly in nature and the *Aumakua*—ancient deities. In fact, the Hawaiian concept of creation begins with *Po*, a female essence of night and darkness. When natives thought of the unfathomable mysterious, it was Po who came to mind. She was the ultimate source of divinity—the beginning of time, nature and breath. According to the legend, Po gave birth to a daughter, *Po'ele*, and a son, *Kumulipo*. The two mated and created the world. It is from this initial point in the creation story that we can see the significant role women played in early Hawaiian culture. The first powerful deity born of Po'ele and Kumulipo was *Hina*; her vast body was comprised of the coral reefs and, later, the various creatures of the sea. Men prayed to Hina as they traversed the tricky waters of the Pacific or went about scouring the shores for food. The name Hina is derived from the Hawaiian word *wahine*, meaning "woman."

Native mythology held the female sex in the highest regard. She was the giver of life, and the cycles of her body were linked to those of the moon and the tides. Her spiritual power was so great, in fact, that *mana*—the Hawaiian source of all cosmic and celestial energy—radiated from her very essence. Nothing was accomplished without Hina. She resided in every living organism, though the crux of her energy was naturally fitted to women. Hina herself gave birth to a son, *Maui*, a demi-god after whom the island of Maui is named. It was believed among natives that Maui heeded his mother's wish to extend the daylight hours, and so he thrust a lasso around the sun to slow its progression across the sky. But the pantheon of female deities does not always begin with Hina. The goddess *Haumea*, indigenous to the island of Oahu, played a much larger role in Hawaiian culture because she ruled childbirth as well as war and political matters. Haumea also had the incredible ability to bear fruit from any part of her body. Life sprang forth from her eyes, her lips, the bounty of her breasts. A part of her is said to born in every Hawaiian woman.

Men also played a significant role in the development of early Hawaiian culture. They were the hunters and gatherers, the protectors. Political power and the machinations of battle were linked to men. Among the major male deities were *Ku*, god of war, and *Kane*, god of the sun and light. Through these deities, men and women alike sought balance in their everyday lives, and the polytheistic lineage of Hawaiian spirituality is rooted strongly in the concept of harmony and accord between the sexes. This is evident in worship. Hawaiian female chiefs—what we might very well call "priestesses" today—paid homage to their deities in temples known as *hale o papa*. Here, women sought spiritual guidance when it came to the cultivating of medicinal herbs or the making of large fires. By the same token, male chiefs went into their own temples, the *luakini*, to seek advice from the various male deities. It is believed, however, that men regarded the female Haumea as a ruling goddess of Earth; they sought her boons before embarking on any journey or specific trade.

Much of Hawaiian spirituality was toppled with the arrival of Christian missionaries. Nonetheless, many of those original ancient practices have survived and are even honored in the present day. We know, for example, that the female deity *Laka* infused both women and men with the skill and desire to dance, and the hula remains an integral part of Hawaiian culture. *Mana*, the source of spiritual energy in Hawaiian myth and folklore, is also regarded today. The pantheon of native Hawaiian deities is not necessarily linked with any facet of modern-day Witchcraft, but their belief system was undoubtedly polytheistic and based in the principles of Earth, sky, moon and sun. We can also trace another highly significant aspect of magick to Hawaii: shamanism.

The practice of *Huna* is believed to date back five thousand years. It is more of an esoteric philosophy than a religion and has been practiced in Polynesian culture for as long as archeological history can trace. In native Hawaii, Huna was relegated to the *kahunas*, or shamans, who invoked the male deity Kane and the female deity Hina when performing tribal rites and ceremonies. The core structure of Huna, while difficult to define, states that all life is interrelated and all spiritual connections interwoven. In simpler terms, the very heart of the earth resides not only in some greater outer realm but also within each human being, as the source of spiritual power. Wherever there is life, so too is there God. The Huna tradition was passed down orally through familial lineage. *Kahunas* possessed extraordinary abilities, and as shamans, they were consulted for many purposes. Their "magick" was abundant with psychical strength, healing and astral travel. It has been said that native Hawaiian culture believed a *kahuna* could resurrect the dead. The chief role of the *kahuna* was not to perform extraordinary magickal feats, however; they were viewed as truth-seekers and wise counsel who offered advice and aided people in finding a physical and spiritual balance. The practice of Huna has grown sporadically in Hawaii in recent years. Interest in New Age philosophy and alternative therapies has reopened a doorway that was sealed shut in 1820, when Christian missionaries outlawed any such practices. Huna provides a direct link to the mystery of shamanism on distant—but nonetheless American—shores.

Hawaiian Gods and Goddesses

The following list comprises a small number of ancient Hawaiian deities.

Akua: the source of all gods, a name for the pantheon

Haumea: female deity, linked to Mother Earth and women; childbirth, fertility, strength

Hina: a female deity of healing, the seas and the tides, and feminine skill

Kane: a ruling male deity; a great creator, associated with the sky and sun

Ku: a ruling ancestral god, worshipped for agriculture
and family life

Laka: a goddess of dance and seduction; associated
with the hula

Lono: great god of intellect, mental stimulation and
learning; also a harvest god

Maui: referred to as a demi-god; can shift time and
earthly patterns

Pele: famed goddess of fire, volcanic eruption and the
element of female destruction; perhaps the most
popular and well-known of Hawaiian deities

Spellbound: The Witch Enchants

Belief in Witchcraft as a force directly linked to the Christian
concept of the devil did not disappear after Salem. It lived on
quite strongly, winding its way through the decades and certainly up into the twentieth century. Stigmas about the Witch
are even common today. But at some point in our history, she
began losing her promise of terror and, instead, adopted an air
of inquisitive mystery. The most daunting question—*who is the
Witch?*—was posed with more curiosity and a bit less scorn.
There was validity to her reexamination in the wake of new and
emerging religious ideologies.

As Spiritualism grew in popularity, mediums and psychics
began appealing to widening audiences. The possibility of communicating with the dead opened the door to paranormal promise.
Though psychism reached its pinnacle by the 1920s, Spiritualist
churches continued to organize and practice all over the United
States. There is no definitive relationship between Spiritualism
and Witchcraft, but Spiritualism facilitated an understanding of

the supernatural, as well as the uncharted capabilities of the human mind. In the mid 1950s, Gerald Gardner's *Witchcraft Today* created a similar sensation when it was published in the United States, and the occult theories contained within its pages did not come across as wholly foreign. People wanted to know about this seemingly new interpretation of Witchcraft. Gardner's claim of having been initiated into a coven that had survived centuries of British ban sparked a revival. But there were Witches in America too. Lady Sheba, born and raised in the mountains of Kentucky, came to prominence in the late 1960s and early 1970s. Her best-selling *Book of Shadows* chronicled a number of occult formulas garnered from seven consecutive generations of Witchcraft in America. Both she and Gardner turned the Witch's old, evil image into something positive and humanistic. Their message was loud and clear: Witches were real people who revered an earth-based system of spiritual principles. There was nothing corrupt or baneful about the magick they practiced. The new Witch was a healer, a mentalist, a keeper of the old ways. She knew nothing of tempests. In fact, *she* could even be a *he*.

Goddess worship was especially prevalent during the feminist movement in America. The word *Witch* was being reclaimed both spiritually and politically, and women felt empowered as never before by the idea of "Mother Earth." Witchcraft continued to gain popularity throughout the 1970s. In 1979, Margot Adler, a journalist and Pagan, published *Drawing Down the Moon*, the first book of its kind to document the rise of Neopagan Witchcraft in America. Much to the surprise of readers everywhere, Adler had met Witches and Pagans in virtually every corner of the country; they came from countless ethnic and socioeconomic backgrounds and were practicing a valid religion. In the same year, Starhawk published *The Spiral Dance: A Rebirth of the Ancient Religion of the Great Goddess*, which offered rituals and invocations aimed at awakening the Goddess in every

woman. The book was a grand success. Starhawk founded the
Reclaiming tradition of Witchcraft a short time later. It was ob-
vious by the early 1980s that the Witch had reinvented herself.
But her rebirth was just beginning.

New Age practices flourished rapidly in the last two decades
of the twentieth century. There was heightened interest in reincarnation, past-life regression and transpersonal psychology.
Holistic medicine was sought out widely. Occult shops sprang
up in every big city and small town, dishing out crystals, herbs
and amulets that promised to bring luck and love. The Witch
was a part of this renaissance from the very start. Rather than
shying away from her darkness, people began basking in her
light. When we study the New Age movement comprehensively,
we see that the Witch falls into every category of practice—not
only the casting of spells and magick circles, but also the reading
of tarot cards, divination, herbal medicine, trance work, yoga
and meditation. She does not escape a single relevant area.

It is fascinating to note the Witch's dramatic transformation in
America—and around the world—throughout the centuries. She
went from accused criminal to quiet healer to modern-day practitioner. Most recently, she has been portrayed on-screen and in
books as a protagonist and not the customary obstacle. She is even,
by some accounts, a seductress. Dare we label the Witch as...*beautiful?* Many have already done so. She is linked with the symbols of
moon, sky and sun; the quenching elements surround her. We
think of her on those calming nights, as the gentle winds spiral
through the forests and across the fields. Her lure is timeless.

Wicca Today

The resurgence of modern-day Witchcraft has been one of the
most astonishing developments of American culture. The per-

son who imagines casting a spell by the light of the full moon
need not eschew the notion disparagingly. In fact, the magically
curious can walk into any bookstore and find a multitude of in-
structional titles sitting on cramped shelves. They can learn of
the power inherent in a lighted wick, the names of various Gods
and Goddesses, even the astrological phases of the lunar calendar. Surfing the Internet, they can post messages on one of a
hundred boards or cruise chat rooms dedicated to finding the
Witch within. Legal organizations protecting the rights of those
who call themselves Wiccans and Pagans exist in nearly every
state of the union, as do occult supply shops and tax-exempt
churches. Major cities have hosted "Pagan Pride" days and festivals. There are even musicians and artists whose works limn the
depths of "magick."

For over three hundred years, the notion of Witchcraft in
America was confined to a single locale: Salem, Massachusetts.
But, as we have seen, modern Salem is a progressive place, where
Witches live proudly and work to repel the stigmas of misrepresentation. Here, Wicca is as much a religion as it is a booming
business. Psychics and tarot card readers line the streets. Popular
shops stock the latest in herb-rolled candles and crystals. As well,
other towns and cities across the country have eagerly and suc-
cessfully adopted similar distinctions. In New York, Los Angeles
and Miami, for example, the "city Witch" is a common fixture.
New Orleans—steeped in the rich lore of Voodoo—has attracted a following of eclectic Witches and Pagans. The
Heartland is home to Wiccan churches, public groups and
covens as well. They exist alongside Roman Catholics,
Orthodox Jews, Muslims and die-hard atheists. Many are envi-
ronmentally and politically active. And many, though it seems to
be happening less frequently, choose to live quietly so as not to
incur the negative backlash that sometimes accompanies the
Pagan identity.

Despite their resurgence, curiosities about Witches remain.

Who are they? What do they practice and revere? Are they good or bad? To some, the Witch will always be a symbol of evil, an entity to be feared. To a growing number of others, however, she is losing that frightful image and crossing the line into a mainstream zone. The wealth of books, movies and documentaries is swiftly and steadily transforming a once ugly figure into something serious and seductive. Being a Witch is freeing. It is progressive and holistic and, by some accounts, downright trendy. Thus, we can safely assert that the modern-day Witch is not confined to a single gender, race or geographical venue. Quite the contrary, she can be just about anyone. I have personally been acquainted with mothers and fathers, sons and daughters, lawyers, police officers, doctors, secretaries, writers and professors who either consider themselves Witches or closely associate their spiritual preferences to Paganism. This should come as no surprise to anyone who has observed the shifting societal landscape of the last three decades. The feminist movement spawned an era of liberalism that impacted our notions of religiosity, and when the "New Age" erupted, it brought with it the seeds of change. People began reaching out to spiritual ideologies that enabled personal transformation. Self-awareness, as well as the physiological correlation between mind and body, moved to the forefront of public interest.

The belief system of Wicca is simple but varied. A short definition might be "the worship of nature." A more in-depth explanation can delineate the Goddess and God as divine aspects of male/female polarity, a conjoined force that mirrors evolution and the ongoing cycles of our ecosystem; here, the spiritual and the scientific merge—and not at all paradoxically. The practice of modern-day Witchcraft is a fusion of old lore and new techniques because it recognizes the timeless resources of the natural world without ignoring the advancements of science. A Witch pays homage to the moon, but she may also employ a holistic approach to healing, counseling or teaching. In doing so, she exercises *magick*—the very meaning of which is prone to misunderstanding.

To the modern-day practitioner, magick exists on every scale. It is born, first and foremost, in the depths of the mind. The subconscious holds the current needed to manifest one's will, but the conscious level discerns the intended desire of a spell or ritual. When a Witch taps into her "power," she is harnessing a natural source of energy. It moves around us every day and at every moment, present in the elements of earth, air, fire and water. There is nothing unseemly about it. Just as we can feel the four elements, so too can we touch the invisibility of magick. Used in conjunction with the phases of the moon, energy builds the bridge to transformation and success. It's like an electrical outlet: when plugged into, activity is stirred. A spell is quite literally synonymous with a prayer. Each calls for a connection to a higher power, and each requires some measure of meditation and self-discipline. Picture the woman who kneels in church and asks God to grant her a miracle; at the heart of her request is the desire to see an outcome fully realized. She prays for change in the temporal world but channels her energy into a wholly ethereal one. The Witch casts a spell in much the same manner, but here, the effect is a natural one because it is invoked. It comes from *within*, from the ability to project an *inner* motive into an *outer* realm.

Ritual also plays a significant role in the life of the modern-day Witch. Communicating with the divine is as moving as it is mysterious. This is the language of every religious tradition, but in Wicca, deity is more than just a notion of something Supreme. The Goddess and God represent creation, change and existence. They are the conjoined source of life and death, the wellspring of creativity and inspiration. They are alive in the mind, the heart, the soul, and in our most intimate surroundings. Ritual honors the Goddess and God, but it also acts as a doorway to a higher state of self. With each new ritual a Witch performs, she brings herself closer to a solidified spiritual identity. The most basic Wiccan rituals occur within the "Wheel of the Year," which follows the shifting patterns of the seasons as well as the balance between darkness and light. Once a month, when the moon is full, Witches also partake of the *esbat*, a smaller ceremony that venerates the Goddess at her most powerful. Rituals can be simplistic or elaborate. They might involve nothing more than a single person and a candle or an entire coven bent on theatrics. Neither is the correct or better way. It matters only that ritual accomplishes that ultimate and most fantastic of goals: a melding of the self to the spirit. Unlike the majority of Western religions, Wicca supports the concept of ritual as an unencumbered journey, a celebration devoid of dogma. Practitioners are free to design their own rites, ceremonies and spells, which commonly reflect individual preferences. In the Wiccan faith, ritual seeks to liberate, not isolate.

The identity of the American Witch is diverse. Men and women of all ages have reclaimed this New Age path, gladly and passionately revering the feminine principle of divinity. The Goddess is an omnipotent entity. Worshipped alongside her consort, the Horned God, she is all that exists within nature. She is also something of a mystery—not only to her devotees in the theological sense, but also to the countless observers who cannot comprehend her emergence in a patriarchal society. Because Wicca is non-dogmatic, it does not discriminate and thus attracts followers who are liberal both spiritually and politically. A Witch can be divorced or separated, gay or straight, bisexual or transgendered; she can practice her faith at home or in the outdoors, as a member of a coven or completely alone. This is an immediate affront to the conservative mind-set; it has sparked heated debates and headline-grabbing scandals and, in some instances, violence. Those who support the ideologies of a pre-dominantly Christian nation—and a monotheistic doctrine—cannot advocate a belief system that is decidedly polytheistic. They can, however, contemplate its popularity with a certain justified uneasiness. America was built on the foundation of our fore*fathers*, one nation "under God" and seemingly indivisible by the conundrums of spirituality. Men and women get married. They have children and go to church on Sundays. Thoughts of God, most commonly, are accompanied by images of Jesus Christ and the biblical teachings, and nowhere into this traditional realm do the powers of the moon and sun enter. Nowhere does the Witch have a place. And yet, she has emerged with stunning clarity. So how did the concept of religiosity change in America? Why have so many embraced a word and wisdom once branded evil?

There are no simplistic or definitive answers. Every culture holds at its core tales of otherworldly fascination and superstition. From the *strega* of Italy to the *bruja* of Latin America, the Witch has always been an enigma, and in many ways she still is. But the Witch of today is real. She has transcended folklore and myth and persecution. She does not reside in the child's fairy tale or on the fringes of society. The Witch is both male and female, fully grounded in a faith that continues to attract people from all walks of life. When one chooses the Wiccan way, she is choosing her own destiny. Wicca is a gateway to the self. It is a craft, a system, a path. Within the mystery and the magick, devotees find a temple built on the principles of self-governance and equality. Here, the mystical and the scientific merge. The emotional and the physical are joined. The God and Goddess are a constant source of spiritual fulfillment. Knowledge is an ongoing process, a cycle of exploration, discovery and rebirth. Wicca truly embraces every experience. It is a religion that celebrates humanity, spirituality and divinity.

The Basic Tenets of Wicca

Though it is a religion that prides itself on autonomy and non-dogmatic principles, Wicca nonetheless subscribes to a number of basic tenets. These do not minimize the self-governing aspects of a Witch's faith. Quite the contrary, they provide a sacred ground upon which divinity is built. There is no hierarchical system within Wicca, no central figure who represents the countless individuals who practice either as solitaries or in covens. I include here the most rudimentary points of interests.

1. The Goddess and God

For the modern-day Witch, there is no greater source of awe and inspiration than the Goddess and God. It is from them that all magick is born. In ritual, deity is invoked by way of these dual aspects, and their conjoined power is infinite. When we think of the Goddess and God, we automatically link ourselves to the universal wisdom. To call oneself a Witch is to express a belief in the Goddess and God as omnipotent and everlasting. They are alive in the elements and the phases of the moon, in the heat of the sun and the rush of the oceans. They are nature in all its incarnations.

2. Male/Female Polarity

In the Goddess and God, we see the feminine and masculine aspects of divinity. Wicca recognizes both sexes as equal and capable of creating a sacred union. It is the Goddess who embodies the heart of Wicca, but she is balanced by her consort, the God. So too is it within a coven. The High Priestess works with the

High Priest in raising energy, opening and closing the circle, or beginning any number of rituals. The belief in polarity between the sexes is akin to nature because everything within nature is comprised of both a masculine and feminine essence. The male and female bring forth life. Their alliance is the basis of spiritual equilibrium.

3. The Wiccan Rede

It can be said that there is only one "law" in Wicca: *harm none, do what you will.* In other words, a Witch is free to use her magick so long as it is not being used to intentionally hurt another person. A second condition to the Wiccan Rede is the Threefold Law, which states that whatever energy a Witch sends out into the universe returns with three times its initial intensity. Thus, it is wise to harness positive, productive forces when casting spells or partaking of rituals. To suspicious or curious observers, this immediately establishes Wicca as a conscientious and humane religion, aimed at self-growth and service to the environment.

4. The Wheel of the Year

Witches celebrate the earth. In addition to casting spells and honoring the full moon, they walk within the eternal cycles of the seasons and respect the waning and waxing of darkness and light. This is an important tenet because so much of Wicca is about the recognition of our natural surroundings as they relate to the Goddess and God. Summer is bright and warm, but everything dissipates with the approach of autumn. In winter, it seems as though the cold winds and steely skies will stay forever, but with the arrival of spring are new buds and flowers and, once again, the promise of summer. There are four major sabbats:

Samhain, Beltane, Imbolc and Lughnassad. The minor sabbats include the summer and winter solstices, the autumn equinox and the spring equinox. Observing each of these days will bring a Witch closer to the magick of the earth.

5. Divinity in Nature

Witches and Pagans view nature as their temple. On a small scale, there is a spirit or essence to every rock, lake, tree or fallen leaf. The bigger picture relates to the biosphere and its ongoing rhythms. But nature is not just about the moon and sun and the magick both can provide. For Witches, nature happens all the time. It is a daily feast because the senses thrive on what can be seen, heard and felt. Nature is where the Horned God of the hunt rules the woodlands, where the Goddess renews seedlings and saplings and freshens the morning dew with rain. We cannot celebrate the Wheel of the Year without recognizing the link between the human body and the earth.

Becoming a Witch

In a high-rise apartment not far from Chicago's Magnificent Mile, Diana Starwolf and her group are preparing themselves for a full moon ritual. Once a month, she and four other women from the neighboring suburbs come together to discuss the Goddess, magick and astrology. They are not a traditional coven. Sometimes, they do not even cast circles or recite incantations. But each of these women considers herself a Witch.

Diana, a licensed psychotherapist in her forties, grew up in Santa Barbara, California, in a "reserved" Protestant home. She didn't feel comfortable with religion as a teenager. The lack of self-expression and creativity in her spiritual life left her disillusioned. In her late twenties, she forgot about faith altogether and took up philosophy. She agreed with Nietzsche that God was dead.

"It was a dark point in my life," Diana explained. "The religion of my childhood was gone and forgotten and I just thought I'd be better off without the guilt and the rules. I was an academic. Everything about my studies was plugged into rationality. My mind was alive with knowledge, ideas and facts, but I knew something was missing. Of course, I didn't want to admit that, so I kept closing my eyes to the emptiness inside me. I don't think my experience is an uncommon one in America. Everywhere I went, I seemed to meet lapsed Catholics and Protestants and Jews who didn't really feel a connection to spirituality. I wasn't alone in my disillusionment."

In the late 1980s, working her way through school and life in a new city, Diana happened by a local bookstore and saw that a large group had convened for a discussion. It was a crowd of New Age groupies. She listened, tongue in cheek, as people spoke about holistic medicine, past lives, reincarnation and Witchcraft.

"And I remember thinking to myself: *Witchcraft?* These people have to be out of their minds," she said. "I was so removed from having faith in anything that the New Age stuff sounded like a lot of fantasy to me."

Months later, at a pharmaceutical conference in Illinois, Diana attended a workshop for psychotherapists and thought she recognized a familiar face. The man sitting next to her was not an old friend or acquaintance, yet she knew they had crossed paths before. And then it hit her: he had hosted the New Age discussion group at the bookstore.

"I was stunned," Diana confessed. "This guy was a Ph.D., a colleague. It had never occurred to me that anyone with half a brain would actually take New Age practices seriously. I went up to him and very quietly asked him if he had been the guy in the bookstore three months earlier. He said he was. We started talking about it right then and there."

The man told Diana he was a Neo-pagan. He explained his spiritual beliefs to her and, upon learning of her own apathy toward religion, suggested she pick up a copy of Starhawk's *The Spiral Dance*. Out of curiosity, she did just that. It was the beginning of an unexpected and transforming experience.

"What intrigued me about Goddess worship was that it spoke directly to women," Diana told me. "There was a sense of unity to it that I hadn't known in any other religion. I felt a sort of instant connection to this spirituality that was noncentralized and very personal. I read up on Paganism and Wicca over the course of the next two years. One summer, I was visiting a cousin in New Hampshire, and she lived a stone's throw from this little New Age shop that had tarot cards and candles in the window. I got up the nerve to go in and speak to the shop's owner, who told me she was a Wiccan priestess. The next day I attended a women's workshop in the back of the store, and it was a thundering experience."

From that day on, Diana began an in-depth study of Wicca and Neo-paganism. The process was gradual but intense. She started having prophetic dreams and psychic experiences. She discovered a natural talent for trance meditation as well. Her understanding of the earth, the universe and magick impacted her psychotherapy practice in a positive way. Shortly after her thirty-fifth birthday, she performed a self-dedication rite on an eve of the full moon. Once removed entirely from the concept of divinity, Diana was now calling herself a Witch.

"Becoming a Witch, for me, was all about seeing the world in a new light," she explained. "It opened up my mind to a higher state of self, but it was more about how I viewed myself in connection to the earth. It was a process of realization. I was continually seeing beautiful things where previously there had been a void. I was also empowered by the Goddess. You can't just call yourself a Witch and be done with it. I think you have to cultivate the magickal experiences and constantly try to live in harmony with the seasons and the lunar and solar influences. When I became a Witch, I became a spiritual person. I became an environmentalist and an activist too. It's had a lot of wonderful and meaningful repercussions."

Despite her own strong experiences, Diana believes that people become Witches in different ways and for different reasons.

"I don't think a Witch is necessarily born," she said. "The women and men I know who call themselves Witches and Pagans come from a variety of backgrounds, but each one holds inside his or her own story about magick and the Goddess. You can be formally initiated or perform your own ritual, or you can honor nature on the sabbats. I don't think it matters so long as a person understands what it means to be a Witch. It's not something that can be taken lightly. Becoming a Witch is a personal thing—one never knows what will open the door to Wicca. No one's journey is exactly the same, and that's what makes for such a rich and intellectual group of followers. When you become a Witch, you're welcoming beauty and ecstasy into your life, but you're also accepting responsibility for your actions and your spiritual identity."

The Old Religion

Religion is, and always has been, about creation. The most common belief tells us that God created the world, breathing life into the cosmos, the universe, the planet. From him, light was born. So too were the elements and the trees and the endless sky. He made mortals in his own "image and likeness" and infused us with the ability to procreate. For this, we give him praise. But we

American Witch

SCOTT CUNNINGHAM

The modern-day Witchcraft movement owes a great deal to Scott Cunningham. He was one of the first practitioners to publicly laud earth-based spirituality, and his unique connection to nature fostered a highly successful writing career. His best-known work, *Wicca: A Guide for the Solitary Practitioner,* has sold several hundred thousand copies; it often acts as an introduction to Wicca for beginners.

Born in Royal Oak, Michigan, Cunningham lived most of his life in California. He was fascinated with the concept of magick as a child. In his teenage years he discovered Witchcraft, and he eventually went on to receive initiations in many different traditions. Ultimately, Cunningham chose the solitary path. He viewed Wicca as a new religion and worked tirelessly to dispel the negative connotations associated with the image of the Witch. He believed passionately in the natural forces of the universe as well. At the core of his spirituality was the simple tenet of union with the Goddess and God.

Between 1980 and 1987, Cunningham authored nearly thirty books—twenty-one novels and six works of nonfiction. Among the most popular are *Cunningham's Encyclopedia of Magical Herbs, Cunningham's Encyclopedia of Gem and Metal Magic* and *The Magic of Incense, Oils and Brews.* A slim volume, titled *The Truth About Witchcraft,* delves into the aspects of folk magic as they relate to Wicca.

Cunningham died in 1993, but his legacy will undoubtedly live on.

also inevitably succumb to the politics and dogmas of hierarchy and patriarchal law. Such is the dominant state of religion in America today: a concept rooted in God as a masculine figure, a father, a guardian who grants periods of grace but promises to chastise his children for past sins. Suffering and punishment are akin to worthiness, and matters of the flesh are best left unexplored.

To our ancestors in the premodern, pre-Christian world, creation was an ongoing process, a magical course of action that honored the earth. The sun rose and set. The moon lit up the night. Cold winds were replaced by periods of heat and moisture. What died was later reborn from the soil, and the bounty never ended. These were the cycles of existence; in them lived the soul of nature. The earth was more than just rivers and streams and mountains; it was a breathing biosphere, a source of life and power and spiritual satisfaction. The Pagans of ancient times recognized the divine spark in their immediate surroundings. They worshipped the sun and moon, the tides and the skies. They knew firsthand the intimate connection between the body and nature. Earth was mother. She gave life, released death and initiated rebirth.

The Old Religion revered matrifocal societies and cultures because the natural world was synonymous with the life-giving properties of the female body. Like the earth, women bore the fruits of existence. They held within them the power to create, nurture and heal. They also shed with the moon once a month. The menstrual cycle mirrors the lunar phases, and this is representative of the female principle of divinity. Wherever there was generation, so too was there the concept of a Goddess. We can see this in Kujum-Chantu, the Divine Mother whose origins date back to India; myth and legend tell us that the universe was crafted from her body. The Egyptians erected temples to Isis and venerated her as a creator. In Sumerian cultures, it was believed that Nammu, a Goddess of the sea, breathed life into the Gods. Greek mythology explores creation through Gaia, the great earth mother. Archaeological excavations have unearthed tomb and cave drawings that depict swollen or pregnant figures, crescent moons and other maternal symbols.

What is irrefutable about the Old Religion is that it provided our ancestors with a semblance of grace and wonder for the natural world. They viewed the earth as abundant and flowing. They worked the land, but they also venerated it. If we look back to those times honestly and with a true desire to comprehend Pagan cultures, we see a way of life that is old-fashioned and archaic but also highly rational. From a scientific perspective, the moon pulls at the oceans and the streams; it floods the darkness with light. The sun provides warmth and enables plants to grow. We breathe the air that stirs the trees and woodlands. Fire grants us warmth and sustenance. Physically, we are made at least partially of water and the fluidity of blood. It is from the soil that we reap nourishment and minerals. We live because of these endless cycles and are therefore composed of them. But the awe and wonder of a sunset, a moonrise or a chill autumn wind remind us of the divine forces that have long governed existence. The Old Religion paid homage to the physical bounty of nature. It also revered the divinity that is inherent in the earth.

Many scholars have eschewed notions of a valid Old Religion. Polytheism and Goddess worship are recorded in the annals of history and in nearly every ancient civilization, but the relationship between these primitive practices and modern-day Witchcraft remains a source of academic dispute. Did the Pagans of centuries past dance beneath the full moon? Did they believe in any form of "magick"? An affirmative response to either of these questions is not at all farfetched. So much of mythology is grounded in the supernatural, and the Pagans surely had their own brand of mysticism. Wicca is not without its new and sometimes radical counterparts, yet its central theology embraces the antiquated principle of earth-based spirituality. It is a religion of the cosmos. Like the Pagans of old, the Witches of today find inspiration and reverence in the immediate environment. The here and now is sacred. All that exists does so in complete union with the mind, body and soul.

One of the most prescient accounts of the Old Religion as it relates to modern-day Witchcraft can be found in Charles Godfrey Leland's *Aradia, or the Gospel of the Witches*. Published at the end of the nineteenth century, the book is a preservation of what was once a dying tradition. It is the story of an Italian hereditary *strega* named Maddalena and the various myths, legends, spells and incantations that she claimed had survived centuries of Christian domination. Leland, an American folklorist, befriended Maddalena on his travels throughout Italy and Europe. Theirs was a long and somewhat magical correspondence. Maddalena relayed to Leland the tale of Aradia, who was sent to earth by her mother, the Goddess Diana, to teach the Old Religion. Here, Diana is the creator of the universe and also the protector of the shunned and forgotten. This applies directly to Witches because historically they were outcasts. *Aradia* takes readers on a vivid tour of what the Old Religion may have been like to the Italian Witches who called forth spirits, knew the voice of the wind and collected various charms and amulets. Leland's research did not produce anthropologically sound evidence of a religion grounded solely in the cycles of nature, but *Aradia* is rich in lore and mystical detail. The curious incantations provide us with a glimpse into the Witch's power as derived from the moon and the Goddess. When Leland wrote *Aradia*, he could not have imagined that it would spark a revival in Witchcraft half a century later.

The Goddess as Mother

The Triple Moon Goddess has existed for thousands of years. She is alive in the three aspects of Maiden, Mother and Crone. This mystical triune is often depicted artistically with three heads, and each represents the feminine principle of divinity. Witches always perform spells or rituals in alignment with the lunar phases: waxing, waning and full. During these times, energy builds to a summit, holds strong, and then begins to recede once again into darkness. As we will see, these phases mirror a woman's body, and also her experiences throughout life. When we consider the Triple Moon Goddess, we find a common theme that threads throughout Wiccan philosophy—that of cyclical patterns and their effects on the human psyche.

The Goddess in her Maiden aspect is young and delicate and pure. She is reminiscent of a young girl, eager to explore her emotions and expand her knowledge. She is independent and capable and strong. Like the huntress, she can see her goals clearly, but there is still much to learn. Her education is one of the self. Everything is new, but possibility and promise are afoot. By way of lunar symbolism, the Maiden is akin to the thin sliver of moon that appears in the night sky. She provides light but does so gently. This is a beginning. It is the first step toward the doorway of power and illumination. Witches commonly cast spells or perform rituals that have to do with new projects or poetic inspiration.

The Mother aspect reflects the Goddess as a woman in her prime. The flush of youth has left her, and she has moved into a serious and more mature state. She has recognized her identity fully. The Mother is all-knowing and brimming with learned strength. She is also the full moon, blasting the sky with a shimmering radiance. It is at this time that Witches give her utmost praise, harnessing her forces when they are at their peak. The energy of the cosmos has been building steadily, going from the tiny mark in the western sky to the bright orb that is synonymous with the womb of Mother Earth. Here, the Goddess carries life and promise and fortitude in her celestial body. The traditional "Charge of the Goddess" instructs Witches to gather on this eve in praise and power. As a Mother, the Goddess welcomes her children into the forests, the cities, the deserted back roads—any dwelling where her names will be invoked. She is worshipped in thanks, and in love and trust. Her graces are also summoned where luck, success and personal endeavors are concerned.

As the Crone, the Goddess has grown wise. Just as women cease to bleed with the moon through menopause, so too does the Goddess retain her inner strengths. She is often portrayed as an old woman, her face worn and haggard. But this is merely a metaphor for wisdom. Having lived life fully and in accordance with her own goals and desires, the Crone is now preparing herself for the end of the journey. Darkness is near. Gone is the brightness of her days as a Maiden. Now she is gauging the recesses of her intellect and letting go of the past. By slipping into the great shadow, however, she initiates the process of rebirth. The Crone is symbolized by the three nights when the moon is not visible in the sky. Witches utilize this time to banish old habits or create rituals that honor the Goddess as an elder. One of the oldest deities associated with the Crone is the Goddess Hecate, who rules death, magick and the underworld. In ancient times, she was worshipped at the crossroads. Those who feared the dark prayed to her for protection and courage. They appeased her influence by leaving offerings of cakes and wine in the woods.

The Triple Moon Goddess teaches us that the universe reflects life in all its stages: youth, middle age and eventually death.

By observing the Goddess as a Maiden, we come to know the exploratory side of our psyches. When we venerate her as a Mother, we instill in ourselves the power and self-worth that are born from expression, knowledge and truth. As the Crone, the Goddess reminds us that all beginnings have endings.

The God as Father

The Horned God of Wicca is as mysterious as he is magickal. In centuries past, he was honored in fertility rites and as the proverbial "King of the Woodland." Cave drawings and sculptures depict him as half human and half animal, often with a stag's horns and hoofed feet. This gave him the rare power to be both untamed and rational. He is the consort of the Goddess, as much a creator as he is a defender. He is also a lover, a protector and an example of the masculine side of nature.

The various deities affiliated with the God throughout history have been revealed as young and old, virile or quietly wise. The Greek God Apollo rides a chariot of the sun across the sky. Osiris, an Egyptian God, holds court over the land and vegetation. Dionysus is the God of human mysteries and infinite might. They are different but share the same inner workings of vigor, stamina and endurance. As a force of nature the God exemplifies the never-ending hunt between predator and prey. His instincts are ones of survival, yet he also brings forth bounty and the feast of life.

The God is vital to the practice of Wicca because he demonstrates union and harmony between the sexes. One cannot exist without the other. The Goddess and God are symbols of the life force that sparked creation, and together they continue the cycle of rebirth. While the Goddess is portrayed through lunar imagery, the God is most often connected to the sun. The solar strengths are closely linked to his depiction in myth and folklore. The God was born from the Goddess. She gave birth to a son, but also to the *sun*. He floods the earth with light in the day, nourishing the forests and woods that are his kingdom. In the God we have several roles: hunter, warrior, animal and mate. He is powerful but never an aggressor.

When Witches invoke the God, they produce the masculine essence that is alive in all of nature. He has no definitive image. A common part of the full moon ritual calls for the dagger to be plunged into the chalice that the High Priest and High Priestess hold. Thus, the male is to the female. The Goddess is to the God and vice versa. As a father, the God of Wicca brings us closer to the womb of the Goddess and into a deeper realm of understanding.

American Traditions of Wicca

There are many traditions of Wicca being practiced in America today. What follows is not a complete list, but without a doubt, each is crucial to the evolving definition of the American witch.

Reclaiming Tradition

Founded in 1980 by Starhawk, the Reclaiming tradition grew out of a "working collective" in the San Francisco Bay area of California. Initially, Witchcraft classes were offered to women on a modest scale, but the popularity of the Reclaiming ways grew almost immediately. Its members have always been grounded spiritually and politically. Today, the tradition is comprised of both men and women who "work to unify spirit and politics." In *The Pagan Book of Living and Dying*, Starhawk defines Reclaiming's style of ritual as comprised of five basic types of concept: Ecstatic, Improvisational, Ensemble, Inspired and Organic. The Reclaiming tradition does not have a specific ruling pantheon, and its members need not undergo formal initiation. Its use of "energy-raising" has been embodied as the now-classical Spiral Dance. The elements of free spirit, ritual and magick are taught and encouraged. As a whole, the Reclaiming tradition identifies political and environmental action as one of its most important core beliefs.

www.reclaiming.org

The Arician Tradition

The Arician tradition was founded in 1998 by best-selling author and American Witch Raven Grimassi. Its core teachings and beliefs are rooted in the Old Religion of Italy, especially those rites once practiced at Lake Nemi to honor the goddess Diana. Structured as a European mystery tradition, the Arician tradition trains Witches in the ways of Stregheria. It views the "Source of All Things as both masculine and feminine." Individual covens of priests/priestesses and High Priests/Priestesses make up the clergy and a Grand Council of Elders. The Wheel of the Year is honored, as is August 13th, a day sacred to Diana. Arician Witches are schooled in the ways of ritual, magick and Nature-oriented worship.

www.stregheria.com

Blue Star Wicca

Founded by Frank Duffner in 1975, Blue Star Wicca boasts more than a dozen covens in the United States. The tradition is hierarchical and mystery-based, and has roots in Alexandrian Wicca. Covens are composed uniquely in Blue Star. Most have an Outer Court and an Inner Court, both of which are directed by a High Priest or Priestess. It has been said that no Blue Star is exactly alike, as many hive off from the original and create their own rituals and practices. Its core beliefs are traditional but with features that are somewhat maverick. Children are welcome in the magick circle, for example, and groups meet on each of the twenty-six new and full moons. Blue Star Witches often define themselves as a teaching tradition, and education in the ways of earth-based spirituality is paramount to initiates. The Blue Star tradition is for the most part handed down orally; there are few written texts or instructions. A majority of practitioners reside on the East Coast.

Appalachian Granny Magic Tradition

The Appalachian Granny Magic tradition is not among the most popular in the United States, but according to practitioners, it has been around since Scottish and Irish settlers came to the Appalachian Mountains in the 1700s. Ancient European folk beliefs were blended with a smidgen of Native American spirituality (namely Cherokee) and a magickal system was born. Practitioners call themselves "Water Witches" and sometimes "Witch Doctors." They are gifted healers and dowsers, and many partake in the practice of discovering ley lines and energy vortexes. It is a familial tradition, passed down through the generations. In the mountainous regions of Georgia, Kentucky, Tennessee and the Virginias, Granny Magic survived through the eighteenth and nineteenth centuries, and so the tradition is largely indigenous to the local populations. The tradition is practical, eclectic, and does not always subscribe to the more formal teachings of Wicca (i.e., magick circles, invocation of the Goddess and God).

www.angelfire.com/nb/appalachianpagan

Correllian Nativist Tradition of Wicca

The Correllian Nativist Tradition of Wicca was founded by Orpheis Caroline High-Correl in 1879. According to practitioners, Orpheis Caroline was a skilled psychic, healer and herbalist of Scots/Cherokee ancestry. To create her tradition, she blended her Native American roots with the ideas and customs of Europe and the Hermetic Laws. There is no clear lineage to the Correllian tradition, but temples exist today in Illinois, Ohio, Pennsylvania and Australia. Correllian shrines can be seen far and wide as well, from Maine, Missouri, Tennessee and New York to South Africa. The core beliefs of the tradition are ancestral—meaning that practitioners honor those who came before and draw on spirits of old in their teachings. They emphasize the worship of Deity and observe the eight Wiccan sabbats. The freedom to choose one's own path is an important aspect of the Correllian tradition, and they regard themselves as individualists because not all covens or groups abide by the same system of practice. The tradition maintains a formal written record of its teachings and beliefs.

www.correlliantradition.com

The Minoan Tradition

The Minoan tradition was founded in 1975 by Wiccan Elders Eddie Buczynski, Carol Bulzone and Lady Rhea. They came from separate branches of traditional Wicca but wanted to create a platform for gay and lesbian spirituality. The Minoan Brotherhood focused on Witchcraft for gay men. The Minoan Sisterhood served the lesbian community. Neither excluded heterosexual Witches or couples, but the root of the Minoan tradition remains focused on the gay and lesbian communities. At the core of the tradition's beliefs is the worship of the Cretan Snake Goddess and the Starry Bull of the Heavens. Many Brotherhood covens place a strong emphasis on the God and male deities. Each group or coven may create its own form of ritual based on the tradition's initial teachings. Minoan rituals differ only slightly from those of other Wicca traditions, and they observe the Wiccan sabbats and thirteen moons annually. What immediately sets the Minoan tradition apart from its contemporaries is that it does not require initiates to follow the commonly accepted Wiccan Rede: *An it harm none, do what you will.* Rather, it suggests that Minoan Witches and Pagans use the Rede as a sort of scale upon which to weigh one's own personal and magickal actions.

www.minoantemple.org

The Church of All Worlds

The Church of all Worlds (CAW) was founded and formed in the United States in 1970, and remains one of the oldest Neopagan churches in existence. Its international membership is comprised of women and men who serve as priests and priestesses, and also as "scions," all of whom help to foster a sense of spiritual awareness and community. The Church initially came together as the result of a group of friends being inspired by Robert Heinlein's novel *Stranger in a Strange Land*. Within the Church of All Worlds is a system of nine circles that build a bridge to personal and spiritual development. Members see the earth and the universe as divine, and religion is viewed as pluralistic. Friendship and "positive sexuality" are also expressed in the Church's core teachings. Interestingly enough, members need not relinquish their previous religious affiliations, so long as they recognize and respect the basic values upon which the Church of All Worlds was built. All rituals seek to strengthen the bond between humanity and nature, and members are encouraged to recreate or add on to previous rituals. Its membership continues to grow because the Church of All Worlds is truly a place where women and men of all backgrounds and traditions are welcomed.

www.caw.org

The Group Mind: A Modern-Day Coven at Work

It was nearing eleven P.M. as I stood at the corner of Lafayette Street and Houston in lower Manhattan. A light drizzle was falling. Overhead streetlights gleamed in the slick pavement. I burrowed into the doorway of a darkened office building and swept my eyes along the wide stretch of avenue. Cars moved along Houston, but none was headed in my direction. As the minutes passed, I got to thinking about the young woman I was soon to meet. I knew her only as Zara. Our month-long correspondence via the Internet had divulged few facts about her identity. She was twenty-seven years old, a social worker, and she lived in Brooklyn. She enjoyed reading historical romance novels and eating chocolate. And she was a Witch. Probably, I thought, no different in her practices than the dozens of Wiccan priests and priestesses I knew. Other than that bit of information, Zara was a complete stranger to me.

At the beginning of the summer I had cruised into a chat room dedicated to Witchcraft. After posting an inquiry on a bulletin board in which I'd labeled myself a "curious observer," Zara e-mailed me a reply. What did I want to know? What questions did I have? She was eager to comply with my requests for information, and so our cyber-friendship began. After learning that she was a member of a coven, I admitted that my interest in her had to do with a book I was in the process of writing. As with many before her, the news sparked excitement. "REALLY?" she wrote in a follow-up note, "COOL!" Tonight, a full moon illuminated the sky and Zara's coven would be convening for a special ritual. Another member would be initiated into the world of Goddess spirituality and magick. I had been invited to witness the rite. It was an intriguing prospect because I had observed only two other initiation ceremonies, and both had proved very similar. For the most part, a woman or man is initiated into a coven by the High Priestess, who simply hands over her ritual blade so the initiate can then plunge it into the rutted ground. Thus, a Witch's knowledge is "returned to the earth" and firmly grounded in the atmosphere. Sometimes the other coven members cheer and clap. In other instances a minor festival ensues, in which wine and cake are passed from one hand to another as the members dance and sing. This sort of celebratory initiation was what I was hoping to see with Zara's coven.

She appeared ten minutes later, rounding the corner of Houston Street. She was small and full-figured, clothed in a purple velvet dress that swept over her scuffed boots as she walked.

Her hair was cropped almost to the scalp and dyed a bright shade of auburn. Nearing the entrance of the building I was standing in, she slowed and smiled. "Anthony? Is that you?"

I offered her my hand and we stood chatting for a few minutes in the rainy summer night.

Zara had been born into an Orthodox Jewish home in Stamford, Connecticut. The Judaic practices with which she was raised gave her a sense of moral dignity and responsibility, but in her teenage years she began to wonder about her future. The life she imagined for herself was at odds with what was expected of her. Religion was to play a significant role in her identity as a wife and mother, yet she feared it would restrict her from pursuing more mainstream aspirations. As most Wiccan practitioners do, Zara chose to separate the meaning of religion from that of spirituality. She felt a mystical connection to her surroundings but disliked being subjected to strict dogma. Worship, for her, had to be a freeing experience that enhanced personal growth. Her Orthodox Judaic roots were the direct antithesis of that desire. In college, a roommate introduced her to Wicca. Zara knew little about the history of Paganism, but began reading about "the Goddess" and found herself compelled to explore it further. On a spring evening in 1993, she sat at her bedroom window before a full moon and felt a visceral bond to the feminine aspect of the divinity the lunar Goddess represented. From that moment on, Zara considered herself a Witch.

"It was confusing at first," she told me as we turned on Spring Street and headed toward Mulberry. "But I knew it was the right decision. I don't know if I can articulate it. I knew nothing about Wicca before then, and yet I felt as if I'd been following it secretly my whole life."

Zara led me down Mulberry Street to a small apartment building. We entered through an open front door and stepped into a dimly lit foyer. She rang a bell and we waited in silence until we were buzzed into the narrow corridor. A staircase loomed at its end. I expected to follow Zara up the stairs, but instead, she went around the landing and started to descend. I trailed her for a few strides and then stopped. We were facing a heavy steel door, and when she threw it open I saw that it led to a dark tunnel lit by a single, dangling bulb.

"Where are we going?" I asked her.

She pressed a finger to her lips. "You have to be quiet or the other residents will hear you. It's only the subcellar," she informed me. "Come on."

The subcellar. I swallowed my claustrophobia and stepped beyond the steel door. When Zara released the handle behind us, it snapped back into place with an echoing clang. I looked up and stared down the length of the tunnel. Brick walls flanked me. The floor was paved with uneven cement. The cold shivers I had become accustomed to were replaced by beads of perspiration. At that very moment, I realized that this was not going to be an ordinary Wiccan ritual. Wicca itself draws its power from nature, and I couldn't imagine any of the four elements existing comfortably in a place as hidden from moonlight as a subcellar.

I silently trailed Zara. "Are you sure this is okay?"

"Oh, it's all right," she assured me. The side of her face was half hidden in shadow. "John, the High Priest, lives in this building. His apartment is really small and we can't do much there, so when it's cold out we head into the basement. It's only temporary until we can find a better place."

The tunnel wound to the right and then sloped downward. Almost immediately, I was overcome by the scent of bayberry, or was it cinnamon? I sniffed the air. The scent grew stronger as we reached yet another closed door. Before I had time to even fear a more confining space, Zara gave the door three swift knocks and then turned the knob.

The room I focused on was surprisingly large. Candles were set in a broad circle, their flames illuminating what would have otherwise been a dark storage space. The light spread gently over rose petals and twigs scattered across the floor. A wooden bowl burned long sticks of incense atop an altar adorned by a white sheet, a crystal chalice filled with wine and two athames, or ritual black-handled blades, a flask of tea tree oil and a black bandanna. Seated within the ring of candlelight were four people, each of whom eyed me coldly as I stepped over the threshold and took my place beside Zara. She made a brief introduction that did little to assuage the obvious fact that I was an outsider here and probably, from the looks of it, an unwelcome one. I found myself wondering if my invitation to witness their practices had been the result of a unanimous agreement. That I might be viewed as a potential threat bothered me, but as I glanced around at this dank cellar transformed into an underground retreat, I understood their fear of exposure.

John, the High Priest of the coven, was the first to greet me. He stood up and came forward, offering his hand. He was tall and portly, with slicked brown hair and a thick beard. Dressed in head-to-toe black, he wore a pentacle identical to Zara's. He was twenty-eight years old and had been a practicing Witch since his early teens. "So," he said, "you're here to hang with us tonight, right? You gonna watch from outside the circle or join in?"

"Whatever is cool with me," I replied. "I know how to cast a circle." I turned to greet the other three coven members. Maryanne was thin and impish, her long hair falling to the middle of her back and disappearing against the black shirt she wore. Her skin was pale. Silver jewelry hung from her neck and ears. We chatted briefly and I learned that she worked as a waitress to support herself. Raised a Catholic, she came to Wicca when she was sixteen. She initiated herself as a Witch and then joined the coven after meeting Zara.

When Maryanne stepped aside, a young Latino man introduced himself to me. Carlos was tall and thin, with dark skin and a downy mustache. He was clothed in skimpy shorts and a tank top and stood barefoot on the chalky floor. Born in Puerto Rico in 1972, he grew up hearing about Wicca from his friends. As a teenager living in New York City, he found himself unable to connect spiritually with his friends and relatives because their religious beliefs often scorned his homosexuality. That prejudice, however, did little to hamper his belief that gay men and women could form spiritual ties. He discovered Wicca when he was twenty-four years old while on vacation in Puerto Rico. A distant cousin he'd known as a child worked at a botanica in San Juan that serviced a large New Age population. Carlos visited the shop, and it was there, amid glowing crystals and jars of herbs, that he first learned about the modern-day Witch. Like other coven members, he told me he had been one all his life without knowing it.

The last person in the group was Molly, a twenty-seven-year-old legal assistant from Long Island. She stood nearly six feet tall, her full-figured body wrapped in what appeared to be a white bedsheet. From the very first, she was giddy and full of energy, laughing as she relayed her own personal story to me. Her peripatetic childhood as the daughter of military personnel had exposed her to countless cultures and religions. It was a brief stay in Egypt that sparked her fascination with Pagan lore. There, while traipsing through the ruins of temples erected to honor the Goddess Isis, Molly felt a connection to the feminine divinity that once dominated history. To her, the concept of God had always been female. In her early twenties and living in California, she witnessed the resurgence of Wicca, particularly among close friends, and began "dabbling" in solstice rituals and the casting of spells. Shortly thereafter, she found herself in an abusive marriage that pulled her far away from the life she had known in Santa Monica. Troubled, Molly fell into a deep depression and was eventually institutionalized. Throughout her brief confinement, she often reflected on the rituals in which she had participated with her Wiccan friends. She began praying to the Goddess and soon experienced a "complete explosion of confidence." It was the Goddess, she told me, who had cured her of her clinical depression. After her release from the psychiatric clinic, she moved to New York and began connecting with Wiccan groups. Tonight marked a special milestone for Molly. On this fragrant eve, she would be formally initiated into a Wiccan coven.

At exactly ten minutes to midnight, the ritual began. The door had been shut behind me, and I sat on the floor pressed against it as more candles were lit. John and Zara sprinkled salt throughout the room. Maryanne and Carlos prepared the altar. Molly, her face aglow in the spreading light, watched excitedly. They stood in a perfect circle, eyes closed, as John stepped into the center and symbolically branded himself with the mark of the pentacle: forehead, right nipple, left shoulder, right shoulder, left nipple and forehead. Then each member of the coven began to disrobe. In moments, clothing lay scattered neatly on the floor. They stood naked as amorphous shadows stretched across the walls of the room.

When a coven convenes for a ritual, it is common to see its members clothed in flowing robes or bedecked with jewelry and makeup in an attempt to heighten the drama of the moment. It was once the custom of English Witches to practice "skyclad," meaning naked, but the vast majority of American Witches favor dressing for the occasion. The idea behind skyclad worship was twofold: it showcased the human body in its natural state and also represented a complete loss of inhibition on behalf of the coven members. Precisely why this tradition was lost to modern-day Witches is something of a mystery. Some say that robes enhance the energy that a coven generates. Others claim that when practicing outdoors, clothing grants warmth and comfort. It is a matter of debate among Witches today because the tenets of Wicca encourage the freedom of sexuality. The human body is a living temple, as likely to heal itself from the ravages of disease as it is to entice seductively.

Zara began by casting the magick circle. This, in essence, is the creation of sacred space. The High Priestess draws her ritual blade in circular motion around the coven and mentally cleanses the atmosphere of any negative forces that may impede the ritual. Zara did just that. But much to my surprise, she did nothing more.

Most covens go to great lengths in casting the magick circle, for it is regarded as a point "between the worlds," where limited human knowledge is conjoined with the unlimited possibilities of the supernatural realm. The magick circle is an important aspect of modern-day Witchcraft because it represents the Wiccan ideology that the supernatural is wholly natural; that the scientific universe is abundant with inexplicable phenomena like ESP and psychic ability; and that ordinary men and women can tap into those energy fields. A Witch's power, as we have seen, is derived from the natural universal forces that govern existence. Within the magick circle, these forces come together at heightened states, and the collective effort of a coven or the well-focused intention of a solitary Witch are put to the test. In Wiccan philosophy, universal wisdom is synonymous with mental capability. The magick circle serves as the guarded realm where that comes to pass.

John, the High Priest, joined Zara in reciting "The Witches' Creed," a prayer-like poem written by the British Witch and occultist Doreen Valiente. "*'When daytime and nighttime are equal, when sun is at greatest and least, the four lesser Sabbats are summoned, again Witches gather in feast...'*" The room fell silent as the last words echoed. Hand in hand, the coven began meditating. After several minutes, Zara returned to the altar and picked up the chalice of wine. She raised an athame into the air, high above her head, as though imagining a sliver of moonlight cas-

cading across the blade. Then she dipped it into the chalice and
stirred the wine before drinking it. John took the chalice and
sipped, as did each coven member, before saying out loud· "As
the male is to the female."

As always in Wicca, references are made to the importance of
male-female polarity.

The latter half of the ritual was dedicated to Molly's initiation.
She was ushered into the middle of the circle, where Carlos and
Maryanne billowed incense around her body. Molly stretched
her arms out wide and closed her eyes, seeming to feel the weight-
less strands of smoke caress her skin. She then stood still as John
retrieved the black bandanna from the altar, folded it over her
eyes and tightly clasped it behind her head. All the while, Molly
smiled and whimpered with excitement. John lifted the white
sheet from off the floor and held it up high.

Zara positioned herself in front of Molly and gently touched
her shoulders. "Here," Zara said, "between the worlds, is where
the power lies. Do you see the darkness now?"

"Yes," Molly replied.

"That is the darkness of your former life. Now your knowledge of the world will be expanded. In the magick circle, you
leave that life behind. Be forewarned that once you have known
the Goddess, she will be forever a part of you. Do you understand?"

"Yes."

"From this moment forward, you are a Witch."

As suddenly as the words stopped, John raised his arms and
embraced Molly with the white sheet.

Molly stood for a moment in the center of the circle. She
threw her head back as she absorbed the full weight of her inner
transformation. Zara removed the black bandanna from Molly's
eyes and kissed her on both cheeks. The other coven members
came forward as well. Molly was smiling broadly, tears in her
eyes. She was now an official Witch, brought to the Goddess in

the magick circle on the night of the full moon. Her life had new meaning.

Zara had begun to gather the sprinkled rose petals from the floor. She took a handful to the altar and sprinkled the petals with tea tree oil. Gently blending the mixture in the palms of her hands, she carried it to Molly and started to rub the oiled petals over Molly's forehead and abdomen. More wine was poured as the members sat on the floor and meditated together. The silence returned, lasting for several minutes. An additional candle was burned for prosperity; John would carry it to his apartment and let it burn out undisturbed. The ritual ended as Zara walked counterclockwise, or widdershins, around the circle, "undoing it, but never breaking it." The Goddess was thanked for her presence and the incense was extinguished.

In the stairwell of the building, I sat with the members of the coven—each now fully clothed—as they snacked on fruit and water. With the exception of Molly, they all appeared drained and listless. "We used a lot of energy tonight," Maryanne explained. "It might have looked like we were just standing around, but we meditated and brought ourselves to a higher mental state. It's a lot of work."

What amazed me most was that, given the extravagance of their ritual, each coven member would return to an ordinary life tomorrow. Zara as a social worker, Molly as a legal assistant, Maryanne as a waitress. John would go back to his desk at a midtown entertainment company and Carlos to the retail store he managed. And yet, none of them seemed to think anything extraordinary had taken place. It was one night inside a Witches' coven, one night in a lifetime of rituals.

Sacred Site

SEDONA, ARIZONA

Sacred to the Yavapai Native Americans, Sedona, located in the fabled red rock country of Arizona, is a wonder for the eyes and the soul. Thousands of tourists visit the site each year because of Sedona's purported magical energy. It is believed to lie on a ley line. The inexplicable currents there are said to be the result of a psychic vortex. Visitors have experienced apparitions of spirits and extraordinary auras; some have even claimed to be cured of diseases or emotional afflictions. A common result of having been in Sedona is clairvoyant dreaming. The intense energy of the surrounding desert is alleged to open up the chakras or induce prophetic visions. Sedona's enigma is timeless, and it remains one of America's natural and spiritual wonders.

Chapter Three

Wiccan Culture

From a distance, the house was unremarkable. With its blue shutters on the windows and patches of ivy scaling the front porch, it resembled nearly every other structure on this quiet street in suburban New Jersey—except for what was taking place inside. As I approached the front door, I heard laughter and voices and the soft lull of New Age music. This wasn't an ordinary gathering of friends. It was a *Goddess party*.

Ani, the hostess, had been planning it for nearly three weeks. A twenty-eight-year-old practicing Witch, she had moved to the area with her fiancé one year earlier. Though she enjoyed the quiet setting, she felt somewhat disconnected from the magickal community at large. This particular suburb was staunchly conservative. There were no New Age shops or community resource centers. Ani often went out of her way to meet other Witches and Pagans, usually making the two-hour drive into Manhattan twice a month.

"It's becoming very taxing," she told me when we first spoke via telephone in the summer of 2002. "I grew up in the Midwest, in a place not unlike the one I'm living in now. I got into Paganism when I was a teenager, and keeping my identity sealed was a tough thing. But then I moved to Boston and everything changed. I got used to living openly—you know, out of the broom closet. And then I moved here and started feeling like I was almost back where I started, which sucked. I knew I had to make a change."

The idea for a "Goddess party" came to Ani one evening while she was surfing the Internet. She entered a chat room, intending to exchange premarital opinions with other imminent brides. She struck up a conversation with a woman from a neighboring town, and, in the midst of their discussion, Ani mentioned Wicca. The other woman, Lynn, responded enthusiastically. She told Ani about the multitude of books she had been reading on Goddess spirituality, and expressed a particular interest in divination. Over the course of the next few weeks, the two became cyber pals. Eventually, Lynn told Ani that there were many people in the local area who wanted to know more about modern-day Witchcraft. It was a positive moment. Ani had long been seeking such an outlet. She asked Lynn to collect a few e-mail addresses, and then started wondering how it might all come together. She imagined a simple party in honor of the Goddess.

"I knew I didn't want to form a coven or any sort of formal group," Ani said. "I felt like I knew Lynn well enough by that time, so I asked her if she wanted to hang out. We agreed to meet in a diner nearby, and it was an instant connection. While I was sitting across from her, I remember thinking: 'If I hit it off this easily with one complete stranger, who's to say I wouldn't get along with a dozen like-minded others?' That's when I knew my idea for the Goddess party would work."

Our conversation drifted through my head as I waited on the front doorstep of the house. Ani had invited me to observe the festivities. When she answered the door, I was welcomed inside by nearly a dozen voices. Promptly, I met the other guests. Peter was a forty-six-year-old engineer who became interested in polytheistic religions after a visit to Egypt. Josephine, a young hairstylist, had been reading tarot cards since her teenage years and wanted to develop her psychic abilities through Wiccan techniques. Seth and Maya were graduate students, earning degrees in history and folklore, respectively. Lilianne, a mother of three, had been a nurse for almost twenty years; an interest in paranormal healing had led her to Wicca. Diane, a forty-year-old attorney, said her family had been involved in Paganism and earth-based spirituality for generations. Lynn was a customer service representative who practiced fortune-telling and scrying. There were many other interesting people crowded into the living room of the house: teachers, housewives, bank tellers, office managers. All were dressed simply. A few had chatted online before, but this was the first official in-person meeting for everyone.

I glanced around the house. Votive candles were lit in the corners, and fresh flowers had been placed in a female-shaped vase that sat on the coffee table. Refreshments consisted of tea, fruit and crackers. Ani had compiled a small stack of information about Wicca and distributed the pages accordingly. In addition to a recommended reading list, there were Web addresses and the names of Wiccan/Pagan organizations located throughout the country.

The guests were sitting and standing, drinking and eating. No one looked uncomfortable or out of place. The conversations went from spells and magick to the occult. It seemed as though every person had been waiting a long time to find this niche.

"I feel like I've finally made honest and meaningful connections with people," one guest told me. He was a young man in his twenties who said he had moved out of his house because his family members wouldn't stand for his practicing Wicca. Here, among complete strangers, he was helping to build a sense of community. He felt "liberated" and "empowered."

A short time later, Ani drew everyone's attention to the foot of the staircase, where she stood perched on the first step. She began talking about Wicca. She pointed out what it was and what it wasn't, firmly dismissing the notion that Witches practiced evil. She displayed a pentagram and gave all those present a crash course in Wiccan symbolism. She then invited her guests to pose questions or speak comments about why they had decided to attend a "Goddess party." The answers were as varied and passionate as the guests themselves. Ultimately, however, each person was seeking nothing more than a positive environment in which to express his or her spiritual thoughts, hopes and experiences.

Much of Wiccan culture is about community—and finding one that will prove conducive to personal development, which can be a difficult task. Geography plays a large part in a Witch's sense of kinship because not every small town is welcoming or particularly well versed in New Age ways. Wicca is undoubtedly moving closer to the mainstream, but obstacles still exist. Years ago, practitioners went to great lengths in forming ties of unity and communal awareness. Some had to go about it in secret; others simply remained on the solitary path. The Internet has been Wicca's most powerful tool in bringing together like-minded individuals. Online connections often result in meetings, the formation of groups and covens and the occasional festival.

Tonight's "Goddess party" was a typical example. What began as a chat between two people ended in a gathering of Witches. Less than an hour into the celebration, the guests were already making plans for another evening of discussion and relaxation. Next time, they would perhaps begin with a small ritual. Several of the guests proposed a meeting on the eve of the forthcoming full moon.

As the night drew to a close, Ani lit more candles and then read the Charge of the Goddess aloud. E-mail addresses and telephone numbers were exchanged. It was obvious from the enthusiasm in the room that friendships had been shaped and melded. Tonight, Lynn said, was the beginning of a "new source of power."

Afterward, I asked Ani if she had any long-term goals for her "Goddess party" idea. She thought about it for a while, then shook her head.

"My goal was achieved tonight," she replied. "People from this otherwise silent community came into my home and for a few hours they lived openly and happily as Witches, Pagans or just curious minds. They didn't have to fear that they'd be scaring or offending anyone. When you think about it, it's absolutely ridiculous that people like us have to even go this far to find each other in this day and age. But we *did* find each other, and that was important to me. I feel much better than I did a few weeks ago. I know now that I can call someone who lives close by and find a spiritual connection. As for the future—who knows what can come of this. It might stay an open group, or maybe some of us will decide to form a coven. Anything is possible, and that's a great thing."

Festivals and Firelight

Pagan festivals began in the 1970s and have become increasingly popular over the last three decades. They are a way for Witches and Neo-pagans to connect with one another; they also foster a greater sense of community, pride and understanding. The typical festival draws several hundred participants. Occasionally, however, a smaller group of organizers will keep the number of attendees limited, depending on the schedule of events. Most festivals take place on the grounds of Wiccan and Pagan churches, or at nature preserves and campsites. Setting is of utmost importance. There has to be a fusion to the land and its natural surroundings before the celebrations can begin. Many festivals start off by the casting of a magick circle, and then progress through workshops, seminars and rituals. It is a potluck atmosphere, with food and drink and open forums. A common staple of any Pagan festival is the bonfire. When tall flames illuminate the night, the ritual dances commence. Other rituals are performed as well, everything from the traditional Drawing Down the Moon to rites of self-dedication and those aimed at raising energy. The point is to get the electrical currents flowing.

Festivals are a magical experience. In lieu of structured itineraries, participants may choose to simply recline with friends and discuss old times; some prefer to trade spells and herbal remedies. In the nighttime hours, a certain mood is struck, and candles light the perimeter of the grounds. Stories are shared. Personal experiences with deity and magick are recounted. These small and highly intimate circles often last straight on through until dawn. During the day, festivalgoers devote time to crafts, the making of costumes or the construction of altars. There are no rules to how festivals are run. Attendees are free to design their own schedules, but group participation is always encouraged.

Jason, a thirty-year-old Wiccan priest from Providence, Rhode Island, has been attending festivals for five years. He credits them with shaping his identity and enriching his personal life. He joined his first coven after participating in an open circle. He also learned different magickal techniques through networking with other Witches and Pagans.

"I didn't know much about Pagan and Wiccan culture when I was first starting out," Jason explained. "I was a lonely solitary. Then I heard about the Starwood festival and decided to give it a shot. I was totally amazed. It was only a matter of hours before I was sitting down with other Witches, Pagans and Druids and sharing in on these meaningful rituals. We danced a lot to raise energy. There was great music. You really come away from the festivals proud to be Wiccan or Pagan or just to be associated with these creative people."

Several years ago, Tina B. attended the Pagan Spirit Gathering in Wisconsin. She had been reading books about Wicca for a long time but did not consider herself a Witch until she connected with her "inner community." At the gathering, she met up with dozens of other people curious about Witchcraft and nature worship. She partook of a ritual, gathered herbs and danced under the moonlight. The experience changed her life.

"There's a big difference between living a solitary lifestyle and living a magickal life," Tina said. "I think solitary Wiccans know just as much about ritual as those who practice in covens, but getting out there and meeting your community is very powerful and very important. It was because of my first festival that I eventually began exploring the beauty of Paganism. I was influenced by the kinship I saw. I wanted it to go on forever. Festivals have a twofold purpose because you learn about other Witches and Pagans while getting to know your own self better."

Now the high priestess of a small, eclectic coven in LaGrange, New York, Tina often participates in the planning of other festivals and Pagan-sponsored events. She credits festivals with spreading the word about modern-day Witchcraft and earth-based spirituality.

"Festivals bring the Pagan community together, and they let the outside world know that what we're doing is conscientious and very real," she explained. "Every year, there are more attendees at the festivals that take place all over the United States. People come because they know they're going to have a meaningful experience."

Recently, Pagan and Wiccan festivals have garnered media attention. Attendance remains on the upswing, and each year there seem to be more new gatherings taking place. This celebratory aspect of Wiccan culture shows no signs of stopping.

Festival Listings

RITES OF SPRING. For twenty-five years, Rites of Spring has welcomed hundreds of people annually to the beauty of New England. There, Witches and Pagans from all over the United States gather to celebrate Beltane. Presented by the EarthSpirit Community, the festival offers many vendors and wonderful space.

www.earthspirit.com

STARWOOD. A major Pagan festival, Starwood has been described as "the greatest magickal event" for the sheer scope of its grandeur. It is located in Sherman, New York, at the Brushwood Folklore Center, and draws Pagans, Witches, and the spiritually curious from nearly every denomination. Here, the meaning of *magick* is truly explored and celebrated. There are workshops, drumming and dancing rituals, bonfires and a number of wonderful presentations and diversions.

www.rosencomet.com

BELTANE. A celebration of spring, Beltane is held in late April (usually the last weekend) in New Jersey at Lebanon State Forest. It is a time for connections and fun for the Mid-Atlantic area Pagans and Witches. Still fairly young, Beltane is growing in size and scope, and the years ahead will only prove more magickal.

www.midatlanticpaganalliance.org

HEARTLAND PAGAN FESTIVAL. This five-day festival is all about spirituality, education and the advancement of nature-oriented religions. The Heartland Spiritual Alliance hosts the event, which is located just outside Kansas City, Kansas. Many high-profile Pagans attend as engagement speakers. There are also several powerful ceremonies to choose from. If you're looking to expand your personal horizons and forge new friendships, this is the place to be.

www.kchsa.org

SPIRIT GATHERING OF THE TRIBES. The motto of this excellent festival is simple: *Leave your mundane worries at the door.* Held at the Blackwater Campground in Windsor, Virginia, attendees will find themselves immersed in an abundance of magick and spiritual energy. There are over forty workshops offered, and the after-dark drumming and fire circle is sure to put you in touch with the beautiful surroundings.

www.outofthedark.com

FREE SPIRIT GATHERING. The creation of sacred community is what this festival is all about. Located on the banks of the Susquehanna River in northern Maryland, Free Spirit Gathering is one of the oldest festivals in the country. It boasts drumming circles and bonfires, and promises to build greater ties to the Pagan community. Explore different paths, connect with the Goddess, and learn more about living the magickal life.

www.free-spirit.org

PAGAN SPIRIT GATHERING. Held at beautiful Circle Sanctuary in Mt. Horeb, Wisconsin, this festival is also one of the oldest in the country. Those who have been practicing for years, as well as newcomers to the Pagan faith, are welcome. Various paths are explored here, from traditional Wicca to Native American beliefs. The event lasts an entire week. Guest speakers and workshops make for an enriching experience.

www.circlesanctuary.org

The Witches' Voice: Uniting a Religion

In 1997, Fritz Jung and Wren Walker started The Witches' Voice Web site (www.witchvox.com). Their intention was simple and sincere: to bring relevant information to the Wiccan and Pagan communities worldwide. What began as a labor of love soon escalated into a phenomenon. Today, The Witches' Voice is one of the most well-trafficked sites on the Internet, boasting millions of hits and viewed pages. It is "a proactive educational network providing news, information services and resources for and about Pagans, Heathens, Witches and Wiccans." A truly maverick site, The Witches' Voice is a free community resource that does not capitalize through advertisements.

Witches and Pagans in virtually every corner of the world have a home on the site. Covens and groups can post messages. Solitaries can seek each other out or make plans to attend the latest festivals. There are listings for occult stores and online supply shops as well. Most significantly, the site keeps abreast of the issues affecting Witches and Pagans everywhere—from legal rights to media portrayals of Wicca. Weekly articles address magick, ritual and earth-based spirituality at large. No stone is left unturned.

Throughout the writing of this book, when I asked countless interviewees what their main source of information about Wicca and Witchcraft was, overwhelmingly, The Witches' Voice Web site emerged the winner. Several individuals spoke of the site's enormous influence and appeal. People told me of how they had found local covens and study groups, personal instructors and churches all through the massive listings guide. Many even credited the site for encouraging the desire to explore Witchcraft, Paganism and other shamanic paths. The most impressive part of the site is the "Witches of the World" section, which serves as the largest networking ring for Witches and Pagans worldwide.

Wiccan culture owes a great deal to The Witches' Voice. For the past six years it has been fusing together the channels of magick and building a history of its own. In doing so, it has laid the groundwork for the future.

An Interview with Gerina Dunwich

Anthony Paige: How and why did you first become interested in Wicca?

Gerina Dunwich: I was born during the dark of the moon—a time when the dark Goddess Hecate's powers are said to be at their greatest—and have always felt Witchcraft and the occult to be in my blood. My grandmother read palms and grew her own herbs and my mother was highly intuitive with a knack for healing, so it seemed only natural for me to be drawn to the Old Ways at a very early age. I was greatly influenced by the wonderful writings of Sybil Leek around the age of ten, and was first initiated into the Craft by one of my older cousins who practiced Witchcraft and also introduced me to Spiritualism. I began writing about Wicca in the late 1980s and was actively involved with a Wiccan group in New York for a couple years before returning to my original path, which can be described as pre–Gardnerian Witchcraft. Both experiences were valuable learning lessons for me, and they helped me to realize that my personal beliefs and magickal practices were more in tune with the old ways of Witchcraft than with contemporary Wiccan theology.

American Witch

GERINA DUNWICH

Among the most well-known practicing Witches, Gerina Dunwich is also a spiritualist medium, professional astrologer and prolific author. Her list of publications is impressive. She has written extensively about the spell-casting arts, herbalism and magick. In 1980, she wrote and edited *Golden Isis,* a literary journal whose readership extended across the Atlantic. By her own account, Dunwich has dedicated her writing career and personal life to educating the public about Witchcraft and the Pagan identity. Her mission has already proven successful.

In 2002, Dunwich published *The Witch's Guide to Ghosts and the Supernatural,* which chronicles her numerous experiences with the Other Side. Actively involved in paranormal research and the investigation of ghosts and hauntings, she conducts séances regularly. She also founded the Bast tradition of Witchcraft, centered on feline magick and the Egyptian goddess, Bast.

Dunwich has been active on the publicity circuit for years. As a respected spokesperson for the Pagan community, she has lectured and given workshops across the country and been interviewed by various radio stations. Her articles have appeared in *Playgirl* and *Sage Woman,* among other publications. Dunwich is currently working with Triple Aspect Productions to cowrite and narrate a video documentary about spirits and séances. She lives in California.

www.gerinadunwich.com

AP: Many scholars—as well as modern-day Wiccan practitioners—view Wicca as a "new" religion unrelated to pre-Christian history. Do you believe Wicca to be the true Old Religion?

GD: The practice of Witchcraft in pre-Christian Europe (bearing little resemblance to modern Wicca) is generally what the term *Old Religion* refers to. The Neo-pagan religion of Wicca is a blend of old Pagan elements, mythology, occultism, ceremonial magick, New Age, Hinduism and Freemasonry. It was actually created in the twentieth century by an English author named Gerald B. Gardner, despite the claims of some Wiccans who have been misled into believing that Wicca as we know it today was practiced in ancient times.

AP: It has been said that Wicca is the fastest-growing religion in the United States. Why do you think so many have reclaimed the way and the word of the Witch?

GD: I can't speak for all, since different individuals are drawn to Wicca for different reasons. I believe many embrace it because they find it to be a nonrestrictive religion that celebrates diversity and encourages an individual path within the faith. It also promotes personal responsibility, free thought, creativity and sensual pleasures. Many individuals who also feel a strong need to spiritually connect with the energies of the Earth find that Wicca fills their spiritual needs. Some people are attracted to its magickal elements, although most Wiccans place more emphasis on deity worship and spiritual development than the casting of spells. And many women who feel left out of the mainstream religions turn to the Wiccan path because they find the concept and worship of the Feminine Divine to be both appealing and empowering.

AP: You founded the Bast tradition of Wicca. Can you tell me what spiritual influences inspired you?

GD: I believe that all cats possess great psychic and magickal energies. Bast Wicca, which revolves around the Egyptian Goddess Bast and the art of feline magick, is a Witchcraft tradition that celebrates cats and elevates them to a high spiritual level. Those who follow this path work with both the magickal and divinatory energies inherent in felines and regard all cats as sacred. I experienced my "calling" to the Bast Wicca tradition while working on *Your Magickal Cat* (a book about feline magick, lore and worship) and doing extensive research on Bast and the cat-worshipping cult that existed in ancient Egypt. I felt that I had invoked Bast through the writing of rituals and poetry to honor the Goddess and, as a result, forged a strong bond with her. She has remained my "patroness deity" ever since.

AP: You have written extensively about Sybil Leek. What impact do you think her work has had on the resurgence of Witchcraft in the United States?

GD: It goes without question that Sybil Leek helped to popularize Witchcraft in the United States in the late 1960s and 1970s, and she strived to dispel the misconceptions and stereotypes associated with Witches for centuries. Through her writings and numerous media appearances, she made it clear to the world that Witchcraft was very much alive and well, and she enlightened a great number of people to the fact that Witches were not cackling, wart-covered, broom-riding hags who had sexual intercourse with the devil and went around eating the flesh of unbaptized children. Sybil Leek, who hailed from England, was the first real Witch to achieve celebrity status in this country and she influenced many young Americans in a positive way. She possessed a colorful personality and a marvelous writing style, and her work (although much of it is now out of print) continues to be a source of inspiration for Witches both young and old.

AP: Your books are among the most popular and widely read on Wicca, magick and spellcraft. Thus, you have educated and influenced an entire generation. What advice do you offer to those curious about exploring the Wiccan path?

GD: The first step is to read as many books on Wicca as you can get your hands on. Take some Wicca 101 classes (most metaphysical bookstores and occult shops offer them). If you have access to the Internet, check out Wiccan Web sites—one of the best is www.witchvox.com. Attend some Pagan festivals where you can meet and talk to Wiccan groups or individuals. You will find that many Wiccans don't mind speaking openly about their Pagan beliefs and ways, so don't be afraid to ask questions. Only by learning as much as you can about the basic philosophies and religious practices of Wicca will you be able to decide for yourself if it is the correct path for you to follow. I highly recommend that you allow yourself at least a year and a day to study and gather knowledge before making a decision as important as choosing your spiritual path. And, if after that time, you feel within your heart that Wicca is right for you on all levels, then perform a Wiccan dedication ritual.

AP: Critics often claim that Wicca is a "fad" religion. How would you counteract this assertion and where do you think Wicca is headed?

GD: I think many of the critics who label Wicca as a "fad" religion do so out of either ignorance or fear; trivializing it in that way gives them a sense of power over it. However, Wicca is far from being a passing fad. It is a valid religion—legally recognized by the United States federal government since 1985—that is made up of people from all walks of life. It is a spiritual path that is rapidly growing, evolving and emerging as a worldwide faith. Although the exact number of Wiccans worldwide is unknown, it is estimated to be in the tens of thousands—possibly even higher.

Of Priests and Priestesses: The Witches Speak

Kevyn Blue is a thirty-year-old technical writer for a major software company in New York City. He is also an American Witch. Initially, he began studying Wicca on his own and thought he would remain a solitary practitioner, but after graduating from college he decided on seeking out formal training. It was a long and arduous but altogether rewarding experience. Today, Kevyn is an initiated High Priest of the Gardnerian tradition. His coven is made up of seven members from the metropolitan area who combine various eclectic paths in their worship of the old Gods and Goddesses.

When we sat down for an interview, I asked Kevyn to explain what first attracted him to Wicca.

"The notion of magick as real and possible and a part of everyday life," he replied without hesitation. "I didn't grow up in a religious home. My parents were Christian, but they weren't too devout. We went to church on holidays and for special occasions—that sort of thing. As a kid I didn't think much about it, but when I hit my late teen years, I started wondering a lot about God and whether or not I believed in the existence of a Supreme Being. I had always secretly believed in the Greek myths I'd learned about in school, but not to the point where I thought anyone else did. I did a lot of soul searching and research and found that Wicca suited me best."

In fact, Kevyn made a list of his own personal spiritual beliefs when he was eighteen. These included a strong reverence for nature and an interest in transpersonal psychology. The New Age movement, he explained, piqued his curiosities about Wicca.

"It was a very conscious decision on my part to begin studying Wicca," he said. "I couldn't accept the singular concept of God, and the more I thought about divinity, the more I saw it as something that should be explored in the present moment. That's where the nature angle came in. When you start reading up on Wicca, you begin seeing the world from a totally magical place. It wasn't just the elements and the moon. It was also the idea of getting to know yourself through ritual and meditation. When you do a Witch's magick, you grab hold of a source of energy that comes from within. That was a very empowering idea."

In college, Kevyn studied biology and environmental science. By the end of his freshman year, he was fully immersed in Wicca as a solitary practitioner. His beliefs were all the more solidified when he realized that he could combine basic scientific theories with spiritual fulfillment.

"I think one of the main reasons so many people are getting into Wicca is the fact that it's a religion that parallels an evolu-

tionary directive," he explained. "There have been books and
scientific studies about the moon and lunar effects. Witches and
Pagans acknowledge that, but we also transcend it. The world
isn't just about science. It isn't just about spirituality either. But
here you have Wicca, and it really melds the two together. It
made sense to me when I was in college and it still does today."

As with many practitioners, Kevyn felt lonely as a solitary. At
twenty-three, he attended an open Pagan circle in Connecticut and started making connections with the "magickal community." He chose a Gardnerian coven. He was initiated and
eventually received his third degree. Over the course of the last
few years, he has combined several other traditions into his practice.

"Native American spirituality is very closely related to Paganism," he said. "It's all earth-based, and there's a big respect for
naturalism. American Indian shamans and medicine men are, in
my opinion, the first Witches of this country. They knew how to
walk between the worlds and communicate with spirits, and later
they were subjected to the same persecution as the Witches in
Europe and New England. I combine a lot of Lakota and Choctaw shamanism in my practice. I think most Witches are shamans
in that they are able to have ecstatic and transcendent experiences during ritual."

The melding of different spiritual paths is not uncommon in
Wicca. Because it is earth-based, it embraces most ideologies
that seek to honor the concept of divinity as dual in nature.
Kevyn and his fellow coven members represent an amalgam of
religious backgrounds that might otherwise conflict where practice is concerned.

"A high priestess in my coven is Hispanic and brings a lot of
Santeria into the circle," he explained. "She grew up with these
influences, but mainly follows the Wiccan path. But like most
people, it's hard for her to leave those roots behind, so she incor-
porates them when she feels it's necessary, like when we're rais-

ing energy. My friend Tom, who joined the coven last year, studied a lot about Judaic mysticism. It's beautiful to see everything come together expressively, and it's not at all contradictory. The point of my coven, and of my being a Pagan and a Witch, is to delve as deeply as possible into the spheres of the unknown. That's where you find the Goddess and God."

Covens and groups comprise a strong number of Wicca devotees, but solitary practitioners seem to outnumber those who worship communally. Sometimes geographic location is an issue. In other instances, one might simply choose to worship alone, confident in the belief that it will augur greater self-growth.

Idanna is a solitary Witch living in Cambridge, Massachusetts. She is a divorced thirty-three-year-old mother of two. Raised in Miami, Florida, and later a suburb of Boston, her home was traditionally Roman Catholic. She often refers to herself and her five siblings as "first-generation Americans" because her parents were born in Italy. Despite Mass on Sundays and prayer before bedtime, Idanna's household was alive with Pagan magick.

"My mother was born in a small village just outside Benevento, Italy, which has been a gathering place for Witches for quite a few centuries. My father grew up in Naples, in the south, and Gypsy folklore is still very strong in those regions," Idanna said. "Everything about us was essentially Catholic, but my parents retained many of the Pagan customs of the old days. We knew we were Catholic but we also knew, kind of secretively, that there was *something else* we were praising alongside the saints and the church. None of my friends' families had these customs, so I knew mine was a different kind of home."

I asked Idanna to provide an example.

"I guess the easiest one would be what my mother did whenever my brother and sisters and I got sick," she began. "We rarely visited doctors. Instead, my mother would go into the kitchen and mix up herbs with olive oil and water, and then she'd go out into the backyard at night and hold the bowl up to the sky. I used to watch her from the window. She did something with her hands, a gesture over the bowl, and she stayed there for a while if the moon was visible. Then she came in and rubbed the mixture over our chests and necks. Sometimes she'd make us recite little incantations. She told us the moon was very powerful. My father made wine in the basement of our home and he did everything according to the moon phases."

After college, Idanna married and visited Italy on her honeymoon. She went back to the towns where her parents had been raised and found more of the same Pagan influence. Local villagers told her she was a *strega*—the Italian word for "Witch." Shortly thereafter, she began researching the Old Religion of Southern Europe and practicing the folk customs that were grounded in Goddess worship. These led her to Wicca.

"Witchcraft felt very familiar to me because of how I was raised," Idanna said. "There was a natural connection to the moon and the elements and magick. I really felt at home because I was rediscovering my culture but learning new things as well. It never occurred to me to do anything but practice as a solitary. That's how I did my initiation, and it's still how I live my life. I've connected with other covens and women's groups, and I think they're wonderful. But you have to be a certain type of person, and a certain type of Witch, to want the coven experience. Covens are like families—you form great bonds, but you also have to deal with politics sometimes, and you have to be willing to share your magick across the board. A lot of Wiccans say there's no hierarchy to Wicca, but it can happen in a coven. That's fine—you have to start learning somewhere—but if your personality isn't of a social nature, then it can be a little tough."

As a solitary Witch, Idanna takes great pride in her magick and rituals. She keeps a Book of Shadows and sets aside her own time for *esbats* and sabbats. Practice, for her, is varied. She doesn't always cast a magick circle or invoke the Goddess. When the

Cash Purchase

Book Gallery
2475 Scottsville Rd.
270-782-7545
www.the-book-gallery.com
8/11/2006 12:25:46 PM   Invoice # 28466
Cashier ID: 01
    ation ID: 2
    Items: 1

    ...Putnam Hurts 'N of Damage
    ..000027697 1 @ $1.99 $1.99

Sub Total $1.99
Kentucky Total $0.12
Grand Total $2.11
Amt Tendered $30.00
Change due $27.89

Cash Purchase

Book Gallery

2475 Scottsville Rd

270-782-7655

www.the-book-gallery.com

8/11/2006 12:25:46 PM | Invoice # 28468

Cashier ID: 01

...ation ID: 2

...f Items: 1

...m\Pathum Herbs Skad Pasaja

4800000228BY. 1 M $1.99 $1.99

...Total $1.99

...axable Total $1.99

Grand Total $1.71

Amt Tendered $10.00

Change Due $?.??

mood strikes, she connects with deity through music, poetry or simple meditation.

"A lot spiritual freedom is what makes a solitary's life especially rich," she said. "I discover new ways to perform magick all the time. I most certainly honor the lunar deities, the Goddess, but sometimes it's more personal than others. When I cast spells, it's usually in the privacy of my own bedroom, and it may just be with a candle and some incense. My altar doesn't look like a traditional Witch's altar, either. I have pictures of my family members, little amulets and charms I've made over the years. I add to it every month, but I don't put rules on myself about how I practice or in what ways I honor the gods. To live as a solitary Witch, for me, is about learning the craft at your own pace. It's filled with moments of wonder and magick in the same way as a coven is filled with feelings of fellowship and accomplishment."

Though not active in the local Wiccan community, Idanna maintains relationships with other solitary Witches and often counsels those who are just starting out on the magickal path.

"When a person first realizes that he or she is a Witch, it's not uncommon for them to feel overwhelmed or confused," she explained. "Almost everyone is leaving a religion of the past, of childhood, and it can be a scary process. I meet many Witches who are spending their time reading books or chatting online, but they're not getting into the actual practice of Witchcraft. They don't invoke the Goddess or form relationships with deity because they think they need an elder to show you the ropes. Having someone to guide you is an advantage, but it isn't absolutely necessary. I always try to encourage them to light that first candle, recite the Charge of the Goddess or just spend a few hours beneath a full moon. There's this idea among many beginning Wiccans that practicing in a coven will make you and your magick more powerful—I see this a lot. But I think the most potent education comes from the time you spend alone with your spirituality. Covens will always exist because they're about form-ing ties and welcoming in familiarity, but solitary Witches can and will continue to find ways to foster their own sense of mag-ickal being."

Armed Forces: Military Pagans

On a military base in Fort Story, Virginia, a thirty-something-year-old man named Pete was readying himself for a night of worship. Back in his room, he changed out of the customary uni-form and threw on comfortable jeans and a sweater. He was careful to keep his pentacle concealed.

Outside, the sky was lit by a full moon. A sense of calm flooded Pete as he made his way to the designated spot where others like him were waiting. Later, he would reflect on the serene feeling and attribute it to nature's mystery. There should have been a little fear churning in his blood because many of the people living and working around him did not condone or un-derstand his practices—he had taken heat for alluding to his Pagan identity in the past.

"I was in my late twenties when I started studying Witch-craft," Pete told me. "I was already in the army and traveling around a lot, so I didn't have a chance to make many close friends, but the first time I told someone that I was a Pagan, the person freaked out on me. I got a long lecture and some ridicule. It's happened a couple of times over the years. I would be lying if I said it didn't bother me, but I know what my spiritual beliefs are and I'm very happy with them."

Initially, Pete thought himself something of a quiet rebel. A conservative mind-set is the norm when it comes to the U.S. Armed Forces, and he didn't think there were many other service-men and -women interested in Wicca and Paganism. But his perceptions began changing swiftly as he moved around from country to country and state to state.

"Little by little I started hearing about Pagans in the military. I saw one or two articles online and almost jumped out of my skin," he explained. "Looking back, I guess it was kind of ignorant to assume that I was the only one, but everything about the military life is done on a strict and conservative code. Deviating from the usual is not encouraged. The first Witch I met was a young woman from Massachusetts. We were talking about a bunch of different things and somehow the conversation got to religion. I told her I had been raised a Protestant and she said, 'Really? I'm a Witch. I hope that doesn't bother you.' I just started laughing. The Gods do work in mysterious ways."

Pete and the young woman remained friends. They spent many an evening discussing the Goddess, magickal techniques and ritual. Pete had performed a self-dedication rite on his thirtieth birthday and gotten used to solitary practice. He was taken aback by the young woman's suggestion that they go out into the night and pray to the full moon together. Exposure, he believed, was risky. But on the appointed evening, the two drove out to a deserted spot and cast a circle beneath the star-studded sky.

"That was a moving experience for me. It made me realize how important it is to connect with other Pagans and Wiccans," Pete said. "My younger friend was much more daring, and she actually knew several military Pagans all over the country. I became acquainted with those people through e-mail and occasional telephone conversations, and although none of us was willing to be a poster child for Paganism, we formed a sort of support group that opened up the doors to a lot of great things."

An even greater shock came when Pete learned that the U.S. Army had added Wicca to its Chaplain Handbook for religious observance. A minor scandal ensued when the news broke, with politicians lobbying for its removal and Christian groups denouncing Wicca as a valid religion. Pete remained steadfast in his beliefs. He did not retaliate when some of his fellow soldiers tried to bring him out of the broom closet.

"I think people panic when they hear words like *Witch* and *Pagan* because they haven't been educated," he said. "When I confronted some of the more hostile people at the particular base I was stationed on at the time, I asked them why it bothered them. They all believed in the myths about devil worship. You try your best to let them know the truth about Paganism today, but you can't change everyone's mind. You just have to go about your business and remember that as an American, your religious beliefs are protected by the Constitution."

Though his spiritual practices differ from most others' because he is in the military, Pete said he found his way to Paganism for very common reasons. He had long believed in the sacredness of the earth and the possibility of magick. He'd had a number of psychic experiences in his childhood as well. To him, the Goddess represents Mother Nature in all her incarnations.

Today, Pete continues to practice as a solitary but has maintained his friendships with other military Pagans and Witches. In Fort Story, he sometimes meets with a small group.

"Things are changing for the better, but there will always be obstacles for military Pagans," he said. "But if people opened their minds more, they would come to understand the relevance of Paganism. I look at it this way: when you join the army, you're expressing a love for your country, for its people and the land itself—the piece of earth you call home. You're doing the same thing as a Pagan. It's another way to tell people how much you value freedom and liberty."

Raven, a twenty-six-year-old Marine, entered basic training as a Witch and knew from the start that her beliefs held the potential to cause an uproar. She began practicing Wicca in high school. Unlike so many of the teenagers in her small Midwestern hometown, Raven received encouragement from her parents and underwent a formal initiation just after she turned eighteen. She attended a technical college and then decided to join the service.

"I grew up in a family that was chock-full of public servants," Raven explained. "My two uncles were in the army, one of my brothers is a police officer, and my mother was a nurse for twenty-two years. I wanted to serve too. The Marines have always been heroes to me, so I chose that route and never looked back. I knew it would be difficult because when you get to know me, you understand right away that I'm a spiritual person, and that my beliefs probably differ from those of the average person. I spent a lot of time wondering how I'd juggle being a Marine and being a Witch. They don't exactly go hand in hand."

Like Pete, Raven did not expect to find other military Witches and Pagans. She kept her beliefs quiet but not entirely closeted.

"I had one of Raymond Buckland's books with me when I went to basic training," she said. "I read it in my free time, which was rare, but people saw it just the same. Some asked me about it, and I explained my interests and beliefs. I didn't get shot down right away by anyone. There were a few hard heads, but for the most part, people said nothing. There were a few curious people, and I was glad to talk about Wicca with them. But I knew that a lot of Marines didn't agree with it. I had heard stories about alternative religions and other liberal things on military bases, and some of the stories weren't pretty."

Raven found support in the Military Pagan Network (www. milpagan.org), an organization founded for people like herself. She started dropping e-mails to her "Pagan siblings" and was soon connecting with them. They were scattered all over the world. Some were even holding rituals in the open, on base or within its limits. Raven was pleased but not at all surprised.

"The men and women that comprise the military are strong, independent people by nature," she said. "We become soldiers not because we have to, but because we can. Because we have inside of us a strong spirit and very high morals. We're defenders of freedom, so we're obviously going to exercise those rights. Truthfully, I don't think people are afraid of Pagans and Witches. Here in the military, the people who disagree with us or want to keep us down don't fear curses or evil spells. I think it just irks them that we have the same rights that they do, and that our beliefs happen to be different from theirs. It's all about change—nobody likes it. There's also the belief that military personnel are supposed to be the typical white-bread Americans, Christian and conservative. That's how it's always been, but that's not how it is today. Nowadays, you can be a soldier and still dance under the moon."

In the last year, Raven has attended three open rituals, all of them held on military bases. One attracted media attention and scorn from the local community. But the air of seriousness and passion, she said, was too great to be affected by anything negative. Today's military Witches and Pagans truly exemplify the meaning of *armed forces*.

Sacred Site

CHACO CANYON, NEW MEXICO

One of the greatest architectural achievements of mankind lies in the northwestern expanse of the New Mexico desert. Chaco Canyon is an ancient complex that once served as a ceremonial center for the Anasazi Native American culture. Archaeologists have envisioned the structure as it might have stood long ago, an array of vast buildings and dwellings that made up a sort of village for this little-known tribe. Construction on the site is believed to have begun in A.D. 900. It stood, silent and abandoned, for centuries, then was rediscovered in 1849. In 1907, Chaco Canyon was designated a national landmark.

One of the most fascinating points of the canyon is its mysterious design. Flanking it is a series of straight lines that reach nearly twenty miles into the desert. The lines never falter and, amazingly, cut right through cliffs and mountaintops and other difficult landscape. Erosion has whittled away at them, but they are still visible aerially. Recent scholars have suggested that the lines are spiritual markings once used by shamans as they traversed to other nearby sacred sites.

Chapter Four

Natural Currents: A Witch's World

A walk in the woods, some say, can put the mind at ease. When the day breaks and dawn's light shoots across the sky, the earth greets us through sound and scent. Mist burns off the grass. The dew is fragrant and fresh. We can hear birds singing in their nests or perching on trees. The first winds are picking up and scattering the ground with leaves and shrubs, rose petals and twigs. As the hours progress, the sun beats, its rays weakening steadily. In summer, the day is flooded with light and warmth. In winter, the radiance dims but prevails.

Dusk settles in filtered shades of red and gray. Water reflects the kaleidoscope of colors and drinks in the rhythm of respite. Soon the shadows form, ushering in the darkness. Temperatures drop. Clouds brighten against the visage of the sky. The moon, either crescent or circle, rises in the distance and signals the evening hours. With full nightfall comes the canvas of twinkling stars: Orion, the Big Dipper and a thousand other constellations. We are reminded of an ending, a sense of closure, a need for rest and solitude. It is all part of the natural cycle of being. It is also the essence of magick.

Just as the earth moves through rigid patterns, so too do our bodies respond to the shift between daylight and darkness. Most of us wake in the morning and retire to bed at night. We feel the physical strain of activity with each passing hour. We are eager to recline and dream and let our minds slip into a lesser state of consciousness. This unending flow is more than just daily life. It is the earth's way of telling us that it too is alive, that it lives and breathes in conjunction with our bodies. When we look to nature, we find the answers to existence. The four elements surround us all the time. Our food and medicines come from the crops, the herbs, the botany of science. Nature speaks. Who among us has never felt renewed by a long walk beside the ocean or riverbank? Who has stepped away from a dazzling sunset unmoved? We instinctively gravitate to our natural settings because the sky, the sea or the mountainside brings us to a place of complete harmony and well-being.

Witchcraft is the religion of the earth. As we have seen, it honors the Goddess and God as creators and creation. A Witch's power comes from the very real and tangible forces that have enabled our planet to prosper. Wicca teaches its adherents to become acquainted with the heartbeat of the earth and the very soul of the cosmos. Thus, nature is the Witch's temple. It is both inspiration and divinity. It is what we are and where we ultimately return. To live by its bounty is to live a magickal life.

The Moon

The moon has long been a source of lore and mystery. It has guided man since the dawn of time and provided every civilization with fortitude and wisdom. Its light floods the sky and also nourishes the earth to bring forth life. Lunar influence is evident in the tides and the oceans, the rivers and the seas. Its gravitational pull affects humans as well. Any physician will attest to the inordinate busyness of an emergency room on the evening of the full moon. Police officers will say the same about the streets they guard, and of how people's rash behavioral patterns peak around this time of month. The moon is a powerful agent, but its properties are still misunderstood.

Folklore and superstition are brimming with tales of werewolves, vampires and other creatures that come alive under the moon's spell. Witches are certainly not immune to these otherworldly fables. The most prevailing of these paints a picture of the Witch riding across the moon on a broomstick. Today, the moon is still an enigma. Held by a clear night sky, its brilliance sparks awe and amazement and glory. Modern-day Wiccan practitioners have transcended the visual attributes of the moon and honed from it the art of magick and the abundance of ritual. They cast spells by way of the moon's phases and astrological components. When studying a lunar calendar, a Witch knows what nights are appropriate for harnessing the forces of luck, prosperity and love or the banishing of unwanted habits and negativity. What follows is a list of the appropriate magickal correspondences to be used when working magick and ritual.

The Phases of the Moon

NEW MOON. This is a time for beginnings. It is during this phase that Witches work magick that will bring ideas, hopes or dreams to fruition. Think of the new project that has yet to take off or manifest itself in an organized manner. At the new moon, energies are ripe with possibilities. For couples, this is also an auspicious time where matters of conception are concerned. Spells for fertility are often associated with this moon phase, as are rituals that honor purity and cleansing. The new moon always appears at sunrise.

WAXING. During this time, the moon is on the increase. It is growing bigger and brighter in the sky, and so this is the correct phase in which to perform spells for healing and health, artistic expression or accomplishment. Here, you will also strengthen magick aimed at attracting good luck and fortune, prosperity, love, matters of the home, personal relationships and career. Think of the waxing moon as *on the rise*. It is a very positive period. We associate this moon phase with the Goddess in her Maiden aspect.

FULL. This is the time when magick is at its most powerful state. The moon has gone from a crescent to a shining orb, as bright and polished as ivory. Traditionally, this was when Witches in pre-Christian Europe rushed into the forests to adore and venerate Diana, the Goddess of the Hunt. The Charge of the Goddess even makes a specific reference to the full moon. Covens gather on this night. Solitary practitioners also set their minds to worship. The full moon is proper for spells that involve honoring deity and the earth, the elements and lunar symbolism. This is also a time for personal empowerment, creativity, communication, conjuration, luck, love, clairvoyance and the heightening of psychic intuition. Because the moon's might is at its peak, there is truly no end to the list. So long as a Witch's intentions are pure and focused and her goals well-realized, anything is possible on this most magickal of eves.

WANING. Immediately following the full moon, the lunar phase shifts into a dark period, when its perfect roundness begins to reduce. This time is associated with the Goddess in her Crone aspect. Here, Witches perform spells and rituals that banish or bind. In other words, one may end a bad habit, neutralize or dispel negativity, exorcise unhappy memories or unhealthy emotions and sever unwanted ties. While Wicca is a religion of highly ethical tenets, Witches do perform binding rituals—in

essence, the practice of keeping at bay another person's ill will or
harm for the purpose of your own protection. The waning moon
represents a deepening darkness and lessening of lunar energy

NAMES OF THE MOON

> *January:* Winter Moon
>
> *February:* Wolf Moon
>
> *March:* Crow Moon
>
> *April:* Planter's Moon
>
> *May:* Goddess Moon
>
> *June:* Rose Moon
>
> *July:* Thunder Moon
>
> *August:* Corn Moon
>
> *September:* Wine Moon
>
> *October:* Blood Moon
>
> *November:* Frost Moon
>
> *December:* Yule Moon

Astrological Correspondences

Astrology frequently plays an important role in lunar magick.
By consulting a proper calendar, one can easily find out which
phase the moon is in and what sign it is passing through. Each
represents a certain aspect of life, as well as a specific area of the
human body. Casting spells or performing rituals in accordance
with a particular astrological correspondence can greatly enhance one's results. If the moon is waxing and in Gemini, for example, spells involving communication or writing would be
enriched by Mercury's planetary influence.

The science of stars is directly connected to human thought and has been practiced for thousands of years. Today, it is a serious skill and a popular pastime. Witches are knowledgeable about astrology because it is beneficial to magick but also intrinsic to the cycles of nature.

MOON IN ARIES. Because Aries is ruled by Mars, this is the proper time for spells and rituals aimed at battling personal issues and combating obstacles. One's willpower is especially strong during these nights, and so matters of influence and self-management are also important here. From a physical standpoint, Aries is connected to the head and face. Spells that deal with emotions or image are often performed during this time.

MOON IN TAURUS. Ruled by Venus, Taurus is a time for love magick and all matters relating to attraction, relationships and romance. Those born under the astrological sign of Taurus have a particular inclination for money, and so financial concerns are best dealt with during this period. Physically, Taurus controls the neck and throat; healing rituals to this effect are performed with much success.

MOON IN GEMINI. Ruled by Mercury, Gemini is all about communication, expression, ideas and artistic inspiration. This is the time to cast spells or perform rituals that involve all of the above, as well as matters related to travel and the theatrical arts. Gemini is a dual sign. It is known for the proverbial "split personality." Therefore, magick aimed at self-improvement is also appropriate here. Where healing is concerned, Gemini is linked to the lungs and shoulders.

MOON IN CANCER. Ruled by the moon, Cancer is the correct time for matters that deal with the heart and the home. The "do-

mestic Goddess" can be invoked here, along with any other
lunar deity. Spells for marital issues and changes in the household are also beneficial. Cancer is tied to the abdomen, especially the stomach. Healing magick for these areas of the body is
best addressed during this time.

MOON IN LEO. Ruled by the Sun, Leo is, obviously, an excellent
period in which to perform solar-based rituals or rites honoring
the God. Thus, any matters relating to strength, vigor and bravery are applicable to Leo. All new experiences require courage,
and facing an old fear is never easy. Here, spells are cast to
counteract insecurity and invite feelings of comfort. Leo is connected to the back and spine; healing magick for these areas of
the body is performed during this time.

MOON IN VIRGO. Ruled by Mercury, Virgo is the appropriate
time for spells that deal with things of an analytical nature.
These may involve career, the building of a business or the start
of a large-scale project. Those born under the sign of Virgo are
methodical by nature. Virgo is also associated with the nervous
system, so magick that involves getting rid of phobias or other
fears is performed during this period.

MOON IN LIBRA. Ruled by Venus, Libra is the proper time to
cast spells that involve balance and harmony in any area of life.
This can mean career, love, relationship, family matters or finances. Physically, Libra is linked to the kidneys. Magick aimed
at the lower portion of the back is therefore appropriate here.

MOON IN SCORPIO. Ruled by Pluto, Scorpio is the best time to
perform spells and rituals dealing with passion, power and the
sexual. Scorpio is connected to the genitalia. Healing or fertility
rites can be done at this time, as well as magick for female frigid-

ity, impotence or other reproductive disorders. This is undoubtedly the best period in which to narrow in on all aspects of sex magick.

MOON IN SAGITTARIUS. Ruled by Jupiter, Sagittarius is the best time to perform all spells involving philosophy, freedom or the intellect. Because Sagittarius is associated with the legs and hips, it is also a favorable period for magick tuned to matters of running, swimming or athleticism.

MOON IN CAPRICORN. Ruled by Saturn, Capricorn is the most effective time to perform spells and rituals for self-discipline and time management. It is also advantageous for matters of career because those born under the sign of Capricorn tend to be ambitious and well-focused. Physically, the bones and skin are associated with Capricorn. Healing magick for dermal disorders and joints are best performed at this time.

MOON IN AQUARIUS. Ruled by Uranus, Aquarius is the time to do magick involving revolution and change. This relates to matters of confidence and self-expression or, on a greater scale, manifesting a big change in life. Aquarius is linked to the blood. Healing magick for any such ailments or diseases should be performed during this time.

MOON IN PISCES. Ruled by Neptune, Pisces is the best time to do spells and rituals for imagination, creativity and emotional stability. Pisces is linked to the element of water and all things expressive. Artistic inspiration is also attained here. Healing for the lymph glands and any such diseases are to be performed during this period.

The Elements

Earth

The element of earth is linked to the human body. It is strength, endurance, will and vigor. It is the muscle of our physicality and also the brawn of our desires. Earth is solid, a foundation. When we think of earth, we are flooded by images of soil, sand or desert. From it spring the trees that give us oxygen, the crops that sustain us, the buds and flowers that perfume the air in spring. Like our bodies, the element of earth renews itself and adapts to the necessary and sometimes inevitable changes in the atmosphere. Therefore, it is also beauty and abundance and wisdom.

In magick and ritual, earth's direction is north. It, like all the elements, acts a corner of the magick circle, but earth can also be summoned when meditating or reciting an incantation. Gnomes are of one the four *elementals*, and they represent earth. Full of vibration, gnomes exist in the spiritual dimension. They are associated with rocks, gems, crystals and stones. When he or she is summoning the element of earth, gnomes serve as a sort of visual aid to the Witch. In legends, gnomes appeared to humans as small dwarflike creatures who acted as guardians of the grottos and caves hidden deep inside the mountains and valleys.

Earth gives form. It is the essence that shapes us. The never-ending circle of Wicca is evident even here because earth, despite its strength as an element, cannot act alone. It requires air, fire and water for sustenance and transformation.

Air

The element of air is about thought, imagination and mental stimulation. Air stirs and spins, coils and curves. It rushes with the snow in winter and skims across the lakes and oceans come summer. It is like our intellect, absorbing countless ideas and scattering them over a period of years. The thought process can also be sudden. Inspiration sometimes arrives without a moment's notice, and creativity can be born from the slightest chance. Much like a quick storm wind, our minds create fresh bursts of energy.

In ritual and magick, air's direction is east. Everything flows on the air, and how one communicates with deity is directly linked to the gales and gusts of spirit and form. Air is summoned in matters of divination and meditation. It is represented by sylphs, who are present most notably in our weather patterns—rainfalls, the thickening of clouds, the formation of snowflakes and hail. Sylphs are the voice of the wind. They circle our brightest moments of creativity, of true vision, and enhance all rituals. Spells, no matter how simple, are expressions of our artistic and spiritual selves; here, sylphs are present when we are lighting candles or preparing to mix herbs. They feed off poetic energy and the mind's intellectual air.

Fire

The element of fire symbolizes the passion and sexuality alive within all of us. It is the desire that burns when attraction is roused, the yearning to experience that most intimate of unions. Fire is perhaps the most physical element because it is linked to palpable feelings that often manifest in the flesh. When we think of fire, we must transcend the glowing red flames and see it as more of an agent of change. It sparks new beginnings and the bravery needed to stir any transformation.

Fire's direction is south. When summoned for magick or ritual, it is represented by salamanders. The human body is greatly affected by the element of fire: temperature, blood and temperament are conditioned by warmth and heat. Salamanders are present when we make the correlation between the spiritual world and the capabilities our bodies possess to kindle new life. Movement, activity and action are necessary for survival. Fire infuses the human will to do.

Water

The element of water reminds us of the subconscious realm. It is emotion and intuition, contemplation and reflection. In the hidden doorways of the psyche lie the seeds of psychic energy and the proverbial sixth sense. Just as the oceans and seas ebb, flow and ripple, so too do our memories and personal mysteries. Water replenishes the earth. With each new rainfall, life is enhanced and cleansed. The element of water accomplishes this sort of purification for our bodies and minds.

Water's direction is west. In magick and ritual, it is represented by undines, who live in the rivers, lakes, wells and waterways of our planet. In mythology and lore, undines may have been associated with mermaids. Undines are summoned for emotional balance and any enhanced state of mental awareness. They aid in grounding and meditation as well. The element of water brings us to a fluid place, physically and mentally, where we are better able to understand our thoughts and feelings.

American Witch

CHRISTOPHER PENCZAK

One of the youngest and most lauded Wicca authors of his generation, Christopher Penczak is an eclectic Witch, healer and teacher. He was raised in a traditional Roman Catholic home in New Hampshire. A number of early paranormal experiences led to his interests in the occult, including a childhood out-of-body experience and, in his teenage years, the visitation of a deceased relative. Initially, he studied chemistry, but changed his academic track to begin a perusal of the mystical. He graduated from the University of Massachusetts with a Bachelor of Music Performance and later founded a band that combined shamanic concepts and contemporary rock music.

Penczak rose to prominence with the publication of his first book, *City Magick,* and has since written *Spirit Allies* and *The Inner Temple of Witchcraft,* with *The Outer Temple of Witchcraft* and *Gay Witchcraft: Empowering the Tribe* forthcoming. He is a trained Reiki Master in the Usui-Tibetan and Shamballa traditions and, in 2000, was ordained a minister by the Universal Brotherhood Movement. He is also cofounder of the Gifts of Grace Foundation, a nonprofit organization in New Hampshire that caters to local communities. Penczak has written extensively on issues relating to sexuality and spirituality.

An Interview with Christopher Penczak

Anthony Paige: What experiences led you to Wicca?

Christopher Penczak: I had an older friend who was in-

volved in Witchcraft. She subtly exposed me to the ideas
of the Craft before announcing she was a Witch, but
I still found her statement incredible. I didn't believe in Witches. I though she was delusional. But I
supported her and was curious why such a well-
educated, rational and creative person thought she was a
Witch, so I wanted to hear more. She invited me to a
Moon circle, and I found it very empowering, but more
important, I had an opportunity to do a spell, and it
came true. Although I thought it a coincidence, it fueled
my curiosity more. Then I studied with her teacher and
learned psychic diagnosis and healing techniques. The
experience was so moving, proving to me that magick
and psychic ability are real. With that and an intellectual
understanding of magick and metaphysics, I was drawn
into the world of the Witch.

AP: Why do you think so many people have come to Wicca
and modern-day Witchcraft?

CP: I think people are searching for something that is
personally empowering that lacks the control factor of
many traditional religions. Wicca is an experiential religion, not an institutional one, and that makes a world of
difference. Every Witch is a Priestess or Priest, and has
the ability to commune wit the divine, make magick,
heal and meditate. Teachers and elders are respected, but
Wicca is a path of personal revelations. It encourages
you to explore the questions you have, and find the answers that work best in your life, rather than claiming to
have all the answers. I also think we have a desperate
need to spiritually connect with the earth, nature and the
cycles of life. Wicca and Witchcraft make such spiritual
quests paramount.

AP: What led you to write your first book, *City Magick*?

CP: I was working in Cambridge, Massachusetts, at a recording studio and artist management company called Fort Apache. I spent a lot of time in Cambridge and Boston, and being a part of the nightly music scene was my job. Though I liked my job, it had a lot of drawbacks, and I felt disconnected from my magick while overworking myself in the city. In an effort to reclaim my magical spirituality from the pressure of the music industry, I started adapting traditional magick and meditations to work in my environment. I did quick and quiet celebrations in parks. I felt the currents of energy in the streets. I learned to see the divine wherever I was, regardless of the urban environment. I had all these practices, and then got laid off from my job and found myself back in New Hampshire, teaching magick and healing, and doing readings full-time. Even though I didn't need the City Magick techniques as much, it did change me greatly, and I thought about others who might need them, so I started the book so I could share it with others. I must admit it took off and became more popular than I thought it would. I thought I would get a more negative reaction from purists, but so far such criticism has been minimal.

AP: You have written extensively about homosexuality and Wicca. Most people would not view them as marginal experiences. On a personal level, how have spirituality and sexuality impacted each other and your life?

CP: One the main reasons I turned to witchcraft was to fill the lack of spiritual foundation I had after leaving Catholicism. I had twelve years of Catholic school. When you grow up knowing you are gay, it is not the most supportive environment. I stayed closeted, and spent many years feeling ashamed, or that I was a bad person because of my feelings. That caused me to turn away from spirituality, because Christian religions were the only ones I had really been exposed to at that point. By the time I got to college, I knew I believed in something, but never found a religion or tradition that seemed remotely similar to my views, or accepting of my sexuality. When I discovered Witchcraft, and learned there were openly gay Witches, and that it was not only "tolerated" but in some groups openly accepted and even celebrated, I was staggered. At that point, I thought I found something that would possibly be for me. The more I studied, the more I identified with Witchcraft and then fell in love with it as a life path.

Even though my first experience with the Craft was good, I know many gays, lesbians and transgenders who had negative experiences because they found Witches who were so focused on the fertility aspect of the Goddess and God, the female/male polarity, they felt unwelcome. I wanted to share my good experience with the Craft, and expand upon it for others. For me, learning that the divine male and female is in all of us was staggering and I always keep that in mind, regardless of the sexual orientation of the person I am talking to.

AP: What was the seed for your second book, *Spirit Allies*?

CP: I had some profound experiences with Spirit Guides giving me advice and information and started studying beyond traditional Wicca with other New Age communities and healers. Although I got a lot of great information and techniques from these communities, they all felt they had the best answer to life, and were all down on Wicca. I realized early on that they were all different paradigms, all different symbol systems, to interface with the same thing—spirit—that is beyond shape and form and tradition.

I wanted to write something about my experiences, but teach ways so others can have their own experiences. I just wanted to do it from a nondogmatic perspective, to show that all traditions can interface with spirits and have meaningful experiences. There is no one right way of doing it. It doesn't matter if you are Wiccan, Christian, Light Worker or into shamanism. They all have ways of connecting to higher guidance. So with that thought in mind, I wrote *Spirit Allies*.

AP: Where do you think Wicca is headed?

CP: I think modern Witchcraft will become a powerful force in changing the world, but changing it one person at a time. As a personal, experiential path, I envision it waking up each participant to a greater sense of self-awareness, connection and healing. As we each heal ourselves, we heal the world and all our communities. I see it becoming more metaphysically inclusive, allowing for broader personal expression of the tradition, but at the same time, I hope our education level rises, so people understand where the parts of their eclectic traditions come from, so they can honor their roots as well as grow new branches.

The Psychic Realm

It is a Witch's duty to expand her mind and the five senses. While it is true that some people come into Wicca with an extraordinary capacity to touch the unseen, the majority of practi-

tioners have to work at it, honing their mental skills at an honest
and steady pace. Such heightened states are achieved through
regular meditation and very personal rituals; these may not be
large-scale ceremonies but simple, smooth methods that tran-
quilize the conscious and allow for exploration. Eventually, every
Witch begins to understand the psychic charge that is alive in
the human body. Quite often, the first experience occurs while
in a relaxed condition, and it may manifest as a premonition or
gut feeling about a particular situation. Later, that knowledge is
realized and the initial fire is sparked.

Psychic phenomena have been with us since ancient times. It
is regarded as a supernatural incident, a transpiration of unknown origin. Extrasensory perception (ESP) is the most common form. You think of a particular person and suddenly the
person shows up on your doorstep. The telephone rings and for
some bizarre reason, you know who's calling. Of course, experiences relating to ESP go deeper than minor everyday occurrences. Those with developed ESP are in tune with telepathy
and clairvoyance, and have been known to predict events and
outcomes or read minds. Studies on ESP have been conducted at
major laboratories and universities worldwide. Results vary from
one subject to the next, but skeptics are fast losing ground in
their claims that psychic phenomena are the work of charlatans.
Recently, the U.S. government has acknowledged that it employed "remote viewers" in matters of intelligence and national
security.

To the astute Witch, the psychic realm is not a distant place. It
is fully within reach and quite tangible. The proverbial sixth
sense eludes a mysterious label in the religion of Wicca and is
never feared. Simply put, it must be tapped into and developed if
the practitioner does not already possess a certain inclination for
the extrasensory. We are not all born with the ability to translate
the unknown. As we will see in the following interviews, psychic

phenomenon can enter a person's life through a variety of channels. Witches are especially in control of psychical energy because it is used in magick, ritual and divination. The circle cast by a solitary or members of a coven is an outer force controlled by the inner workings of the mind; conducting this rite and working magick between the worlds comprise a journey into the psychic realm. Divinity in nature is yet another example—in worshipping the power of the earth, we are harnessing its hidden potentials and opening the mind to greater depths. The psychic realm is around us at all times.

Cory: Near Death

In February 1996, Cory, a second-degree Witch living in Des Moines, Iowa, was driving home from a friend's house in the middle of a winter storm. It was nothing new. He had been raised in a fairly rural community and was accustomed to wild bursts of weather. On this particular night, however, conditions were especially treacherous. The temperature had dropped considerably, and black ice gleamed on the tarmac. The ride would be rough.

Cory was nineteen at the time. It is important to note that he had been raised in an agnostic home. He knew nothing about Wicca or the New Age practices already afoot in America.

"When telling my story, I think it's important for people to know how removed I was from anything supernatural," Cory told me. "You always hear stories about those New Age groupies who take a fall or get struck by lightning and then end up with weird powers. But that's not me. Up until that night in February, I thought anything related to the occult was nonsense."

That night, Cory's mind was focused on getting home. He drove at a normal pace, just beneath the speed limit. When he reached the section of highway flanked by woodland, he instinctively slowed down. The darkness was total. Snow was falling and a furious wind whipped through the trees. Keeping one hand on the wheel, Cory leaned slightly to one side to retrieve a cigarette from the glove compartment. His eyes left the road for a single moment. It was a moment that ultimately changed his life.

"A car was speeding up from the opposite lane and I didn't see it," Cory explained. "Before I knew what was happening, the car cut me off to make an exit, and I hit the brakes and started swerving. The world never looked so animated."

Cory's car slid off the road and spun into the woods, crashing through trees and bushes. The impact was stunning.

"I remember screaming and trying to get control of the wheel, but it happened very fast," Cory said. "I never saw the tree that I slammed into. I don't remember any of that. There was blunt trauma to my head upon impact and I lost consciousness, and that's when I died."

Cory used the word *died* to explain what had happened to "his old self" at the moment of impact. The godless, spiritually disinterested kid slipped away forever in the wake of an extraordinary experience.

"All of a sudden, I opened my eyes and understood what had happened. I saw glass and blood everywhere, but I didn't feel anything. When I looked up, I was instantly looking down, back at myself and the accident scene. I was floating above it. I saw myself strapped into the car seat. I didn't recognize my own face because of the injuries, and the funny thing is that I remember thinking to myself that I had been wrong about life and death, because there I was, staring down at my dead body. But I was alive in another way. I had never felt so free and full as in those moments."

Cory then described what has become a common pattern in the near-death experience: a sense of flying, a colorful vortex, and an indescribably bright light drawing him in. He also felt—but did not hear—an inner voice speaking to him.

"I can't really describe the voice," he said. "But I know that in the middle of the experience, something was letting me know that I wasn't going into the light, that I was instead going to return back to where I had been before. And that's what happened."

In essence, Cory had returned to the accident scene. He watched as the dark road was illuminated by lights and sirens. He watched his own broken body being pulled from the twisted steel. In the ambulance, he listened as paramedics shouted commands and called him a "flatliner." One of the paramedics, a middle-aged woman, looked down at Cory as he lay strapped in the stretcher and said the words: *Oh God, he looks just like my nephew, Steven.*

When Cory woke, it was early the next day. He had suffered a skull fracture and several internal lacerations. His recovery lasted nearly six months. By then, he was a changed person and didn't quite know what to make of his otherworldly journey. Not surprisingly, his parents chided him. Most of his friends told him it was merely a result of the impact. But Cory knew better. He had undergone something real, and it wasn't letting him go. Within a year of the accident, he began having prophetic dreams and intense psychic experiences.

"I first dreamed of my Uncle Tom, who we all knew was having marital problems," Cory explained. "I dreamed very clearly that he was going to be a father, and that the child would be a boy. It was so real to me that I called and told him about it a few days later. He thought I was losing it, but two months later, his wife announced that she was pregnant. It was miracle because they had been trying to conceive for almost five years and given up hope. My little cousin, a boy, was born right on schedule and as predicted."

But even before the child's birth, Cory was struggling to understand his other uncanny abilities, especially his knack for pinpointing the whereabouts of certain individuals at far distances. He had developed a strange reputation among the members of his family. The more he tried to ignore them, the stronger his psychic skills grew. Soon, he was seeing auras around people if he stared at them for longer than a minute. The unexplained realities, coupled with the memory of his near-death experience, led him to research. He read every book he could find on psychic phenomena. Slowly but surely, he came to accept his abilities but felt set apart from his surroundings. In secret, he began forming relationships with the adherents of a Spiritualist church, where he was encouraged to explore ESP and mediumship. He had remarkable success.

"I can't explain what happened to me," Cory said, "but I believe that my walk on the Other Side blew open a few passageways in my brain. Something inside of me is just more receptive to energy now. It's been a few years, but it still amazes me. I absolutely believe in a supreme being now, and that nature is a sacred realm unto itself. It's all here. There's not a complete division between this world and the next. Mine is a common conclusion where near-death experiences are concerned. People who've 'seen the light' frequently develop psychic abilities or a heightened sense of the world around them."

Cory never forgot what transpired in the ambulance on the night of his accident, and he eventually tracked down the female paramedic who had worked to bring him back from the trenches of death. They met. She remembered Cory clearly. When he asked her if he still looked like her nephew, Steven, the woman was stunned. Her recollection was anything but vague. She had, in fact, spoken those very words while performing CPR on Cory. It only served to confirm his sojourn into an uncharted, ethereal realm.

Two years ago, Cory began studying Wicca. He is now a second-degree initiate in the Gardnerian tradition. His psychic abilities continue to lead him—and others—in new and enlightening directions.

Danielle: Second, Spirited Sight

As a child, Danielle hated playing with the other kids in her suburban Chicago neighborhood. She had no interest in dolls, swing sets or the nearest park. Her world was already populated by adults. Most of them never spoke, nor did they tell her their names. They simply stared at her in amazement, as if unable to believe she could actually *see* them.

"I had an indistinct sense that something was different about the people I would glimpse," Danielle, a thirty-six-year-old fashion stylist, said. "They weren't as animated as my parents and aunts and uncles, I guess you'd say. The spirits always looked like they were behind a filmy curtain, and they were silent. Sometimes they would stare at me and then vanish, and then there were the rare times when one would stand beside me and just wait. I don't remember when it all started because I've been this way all my life."

It was when Danielle got to school that she realized something was terribly wrong. She would point to people nobody else could see, and she seemed to know what her teachers were going to say or do before they said or did anything. Her abilities did not go over well with people.

"I had no way of explaining my sight to my parents," she said. "They would sit down with me and ask me questions, alluding to trickery on my part. They didn't believe in psychic phenomena or an earthbound spirit realm. In their minds, people died and went to heaven, and that was that. But by the time I was eight, I understood that the dead lived around us and that for some reason, I was able to see them. I was born with this sixth sense. I've been doing it all my life."

In her teenage years, Danielle was dubbed the school outcast. Though never the brunt of jokes, other students did not want to be around her much—except on Halloween. They called her a Witch. She hated the label because it conjured negative images.

"At the time, I thought being called a Witch was the worst possible thing," she said. "People cringed at the word and thought of satanic things. I didn't want to be attached to that label because my parents were very Christian people."

Not surprisingly, Danielle spent many years trying to ignore her psychic sight, but there was no escaping it. She saw the spirit world all around her. She was unable to comprehend the enormity of her gift and began believing the image other people had of her. Why was she such a freak? Why couldn't she act like a normal person? The inner turmoil led to a bout with depression, and at the tender age of seventeen, Danielle was psychiatrically evaluated.

"It was a dangerous time in my life because I knew what would happen if I admitted to a doctor that I was seeing people appear and disappear before my eyes," she explained. "I never thought I was crazy or losing my sanity because, as I've said, it's been this way for me since childhood. But I didn't want to be locked up for schizophrenia. After a few long chat sessions, things calmed down and I just resigned myself to the fact that I had been cursed, that this was my cross in life. I was uncomfortable in my own skin."

But in her senior year of high school, something happened that changed Danielle's perceptions about her abilities and herself. It was a windy winter day. She and a few other girls had stayed after class to help their teachers decorate the gymnasium for an upcoming Valentine's Day event. The school had installed a heavy, large heart-shaped sculpture in the center of the floor. It was several feet tall. A few of the girls had begun adorning it with roses and garlands, some of them perched on a ladder. Suddenly, Danielle was seized by a terrible feeling.

"I was standing on the opposite side of the floor," she explained. "Out of nowhere, I started to shake and became overwhelmed by a sense of danger. My heart started beating very fast. I knew something awful was about to happen so I screamed for the girls to get away from the sculpture. I was pretty crazed. One of the teachers came over to me and tried to calm me down, but thankfully, the girls listened and moved away."

A moment later, they all watched as the sculpture came crashing down to the floor. It had not been secured properly and tipped over. There was a massive clatter. Had anyone been standing beneath it, the results would have been tragic.

"It was silent for a long time after that. No one could believe what had happened," Danielle said. "People just stood there, staring at me and what was left of the sculpture. It actually made a dent into the floor. Those girls would have been killed or very severely injured had I not spoken up. After that, everyone started calling me 'Carrie,' but for the first time in my life, I understood that my abilities could have a positive outcome. It was all about learning how to use them."

While in college, Danielle was the subject of a private ESP experiment at the University of Chicago. She was administered various tests. It was discovered that her brain wave activity superseded that of the average person. While sitting in a windowless room, she accurately described what other experiment participants were drawing elsewhere seven out of nine times.

Throughout her twenties, Danielle embarked on a personal journey into the heart of her psychic abilities, speaking to mediums and researchers and paranormal investigators. She developed her mediumistic skills with the intention of helping those who have lost loved ones, especially parents. She views psychic ability as a rare yet natural occurrence. She does not believe all people can tap into it completely. ESP can be developed, she said, but only to a certain degree. Communication with the dead, according to Danielle, is an innate skill.

"I believe that those who have passed over can still make themselves known in the physical world," she said. "But being able to help them in that mission is a natural gift. You have to be born with some measure of capability. As for my own spiritual beliefs, I guess I would call myself a reluctant Witch. I don't practice Wicca, but I identify with the image of the Witch as a healer and knower of hidden things. It's taken me a long time to understand psychic ability. After all these years, I can honestly say that I feel blessed, especially when I know I've helped someone through the grieving process. If I had one message to impart it would be that we don't die."

Today, Danielle works a "normal, nine-to-five job," but she administers to those in need of her psychic abilities regularly.

Margaret: The Psychic's Path

When she was twenty-five-years-old, Margaret, of Portland, Maine, began studying Wicca. She read books and slowly started practicing magick, but her efforts did not yield fruitful results. She consulted an astrological calendar for the appropriate phases of the moon. She made a color chart to remind her of which candles would work best. But nothing seemed to create the needed spark.

"I felt very stagnant in all of my magickal workings, and I just couldn't understand what I was doing wrong," Margaret explained. "The more books I read, the more confused I became. There are thousands of methods for casting spells and invoking the Gods, and that kind of information overload can be misleading. When I really sat down and questioned myself, I realized that I wasn't connecting psychically to my own energy. I had never had any kind of paranormal experiences in the past, but I believed myself capable of reaching that altered state."

She decided to concentrate on her preparation techniques. Instead of simply gathering materials for a particular spell, she spent an ample amount of time grounding and centering her energy beforehand.

"I was blocked, so I didn't perform any magick for quite a few months," she said. "Instead, I would use the nights of the full moon to meditate on my desire to learn psychism and maybe a little ESP. I had read stories about ordinary people who developed psychic abilities after a lot of practice. The majority of the Witches and mediums I knew all agreed that it was something that could be attained."

Visualization worked best for Margaret. She spent one hour three evenings a week visualizing the inner workings of her brain—the blood vessels, cells and nerves. She imagined them "opening up and receiving astral light." Later, she practiced with ordinary playing cards, psychically discerning which would show up from a blind deck. Within two months, she noticed a change.

"When you are training yourself for psychic ability, you begin to see the mind as a radar," she explained. "I noticed a significant difference in my senses, in the way I was seeing my surroundings and picking up on things that other people didn't. I also started experiencing strange personal phenomena. I knew when certain people I hadn't heard from in a while were going to call. I would go places I had never been to before without any directions—I let my senses guide me instead. It wasn't easy, and I had periods where I experienced severe blocks, but positive changes were taking place and my abilities as a Witch were strengthening."

Margaret was especially influenced by the life and work of Edgar Cayce, one of the most renowned psychics of our time. Cayce practiced absent healing, a technique by which he psychically healed people from great distances. In an unconscious state, he was able to diagnose illness and prescribe effective treatments. Like Cayce, although his rare ability had been spontaneous since birth, Margaret eventually began working as a psychic healer, using her own honed skills and a "supernaturally scientific method." She had never studied medicine, but her accuracy when working with patients on a private basis proved astounding.

"I begin psychic diagnosis by first laying my hands over a person's solar plexus," she explained. "Then I begin my own visualization, and I mentally see inside the person's body, letting intuition guide me. When I hit on the afflicted area, my mind freezes in on it. I'm often able to diagnose an ailment accurately before a doctor does. That helps in treatment. I tell people that the best cure for anything is to first be aware of the connection between our minds and our bodies."

Margaret is of the theory that anyone can develop psychic ability. She credits a disciplined, streamlined approach to her success. Meditation and visualization are key to awakening the mind's powers. As a Witch, her magickal practices have reaped the rewards of her intuitive nature.

Divination

The art of fortune-telling has existed in every culture throughout history. It was—and still is—used to locate lost objects or people, solve problems and predict future events. Witches become expert diviners with practice and often use their skills to aid others or enhance personal development. One can divine for any aspect of life: home, love, career, health, protection and physical needs. Like all magick, it is an endless fount of energy and knowledge.

Divination takes many forms. The most common are astrology, the tarot and numerology. Channeling—the act of communicating with spirits directly—is also a form of divination. In ancient times, soothsayers used runes and various signs and symbols to unearth the will of the Gods. These are still common today, as is palmistry and the use of the Ouija board. As with any magick, it is important to exercise caution and responsibility when working with the psychic and spirit realms.

Tasseography

Otherwise known as the reading of tea leaves, tasseography is an ancient custom believed to have originated with the Gypsy tribes of Eastern Europe. This form of divination works with the shapes that are left by tea leaves either on the rim, or the bottom, of a cup.

First, you ask the person for whom you are divining to drink the tea until only a bit of it is left. Next, you ask the person to rotate the cup clockwise two or three times. Finally, the cup should be turned over by the drinker, onto the saucer, to allow the excess liquid to drain. What follows is a list of the most common symbols made by the tea leaves and their meanings:

Apple: Indicates the Goddess and a desire to explore spirituality. Also represents motherhood and childbirth.
Bat: An omen of ill fortune and a symbol of darkness. It may also represent the unresolved issues of the subconscious mind.
Bell: Traditionally tied to weddings and marriage, though it can augur the start of a significant new relationship
Bird: Symbolizes ambition and success in business ventures.
Butterfly: An indication of dishonesty in a partnership. It also symbolizes a change in life, a movement of some sort.
Cat: A two-sided symbol. It can indicate problems in the

home if the face is barely visible, but a clear image represents serenity in domestic life.

Cornstalk: Symbolizes virility and a connection to the masculine. For women, this may indicate passion in a relationship; for men, the symbol represents the start of a new
relationship.

Cross: An image of difficulty or strife. This traditional image
of a cross represents a heavy emotional weight, a strain on
the mind and the well-being.

Crossroads: Indicates a need for direction in life; a symbol
sacred to the Goddess Hecate.

Dagger: A symbol of betrayal and distrust.

Dog: A positive symbol indicating harmony and a strong
personal bond between two people.

Earth: A circular globe symbolizing Earth, indicative of a
higher state of self-knowledge and confidence, possibly
achieved through education or travel.

Frog: An omen of good luck, especially in health.

Gun: Symbolizes danger. If the barrel is clearly pointing
south, it indicates the ending of a turbulent relationship
or time.

Hand: Indicates the need for help in a pressing or trying
situation.

Heart: The eternal symbol of love. A broken or cracked heart
represents a sense of mourning and pain.

Leaf: A symbol of peace and harmony and a desire to leave
the past behind. Indicates letting go and moving forward.

The Tarot

A centuries-old system of divination, the tarot deck consists of
seventy-eight cards: twenty-two in the Major Arcana and fifty-

six in the Minor Arcana. The seeker, or the one who wishes to consult the cards, must keep a question in mind while his or her cards are being read. In certain instances, the cards may be used without a traditional "spread."

THE MAJOR ARCANA

The Fool: A card of beginnings, of journeys and of innocence

The Magician: A card of guidance, skill and creativity

The High Priestess: A card of spiritual depth, intuition, the psychic realm

The Empress: A card of inner growth and knowledge, a sense of nurturing

The Emperor: A card of responsibility, leadership and authority

The Hierophant: A card of spiritual wisdom, tradition and convention

The Lovers: A card of choice, action, love and inspiration

The Chariot: A card of life's direction, victory and success

Strength: A card of will, determination and inner peace

The Hermit: A card of silence and withdrawal, and also of truth

Wheel of Fortune: A card of fate, random fortune, luck

Justice: A card of judgment, fairness, weight of decisions

The Hanged Man: A card of self-sacrifice, and also of discharge

Death: A card of transformation, change, renewal

Temperance: A card of healing, patience and harmony

The Devil: A card of temptation, seduction, pride

The Tower: A card of change and surprises, occasionally of upheaval

The Star: A card of prospects and faith, of one's personal dreams

The Moon: A card of intuition, reason and revelation
The Sun: A card of fulfillment and accomplishment
Judgment A card of awakening and lucidity
The World: A card of triumph, success and achievement

Spiritual Science: Healing

Paul lived a relatively quiet, lonesome life. Many of his friends and coworkers were not aware of his identity as a Witch. The day we met, he wore chinos and a T-shirt; I sought out but found no pentacles or crystals dangling from his neck, and all ten of his fingers were devoid of rings. He identified him as a "spiritualist healer and steadfast scientist."

"Contrary to popular belief, science and spirituality can complement each other very well," Paul explained. "You can see that in a lot of Eastern thought and philosophy, but it's very true in Wicca."

In the main, Paul spent his days working as a registered nurse at a hospital in Newport, Rhode Island, and his nights reading in the privacy of his modest home. Though nearing forty, he had a boyish look about him. What made Paul a Witch was his belief that life should be lived in accordance with the natural cycles and rhythms of the earth.

He seemed an interesting dichotomy, for he expertly wove the scientific and the metaphysical together. He spoke a great deal about the moon's biological effects on the human body and the world as a whole. He pointed out that certain diseases were diagnosed in higher rates at various intervals throughout the year, depending on how much light or darkness the atmosphere absorbed. Medicine in its purest herbal form, he said, was the most effective medical treatment any patient could undergo.

When I suggested that he posed a conflict as both scientist and Witch, he merely shook his head. "To me, it makes perfect sense. It all goes hand in hand. The human body itself is made up of the earth, and Wicca reveres the earth. Witches are healers. They were the first doctors and scientists of the world because they recognized the fusion of mind, body and spirit."

As a nurse and holistic counselor, Paul sought to treat patients completely, focusing his attention on their physical and spiritual needs. He was known in the hospital as the "New Age Nightingale." Oftentimes, he could be found making the rounds in the intensive care unit after patients had been administered their daily dose of medication. With their permission, he frequently enhanced treatment with aromatherapy or New Age music. The practice of Wicca was especially important in his life because it gave him a concise understanding of the cycle of death and rebirth. Death, by his own estimation, was as natural a process as birth. Paul saw demise on a daily basis, but it never embittered him. Rather, it reminded him of the intimate connection between human physiology and nature.

"That's a common trait among modern-day Witches," he said. "We don't fear death. Dying is simply a gateway into another continuum of eternity. Life and death go hand in hand because they are part of the never-ending cycle that comprises existence. Plant life, for example, dies in winter but is renewed with the approach of spring. Witches see human life as mirroring this course. What goes up, in essence, must come down. As above, so below."

The realist rationale has helped Paul with the daily grind of his job.

"When I see death," he said, "I'm reminded of how the Pagans of pre-Christian Europe celebrated a loved one's departure because it meant the soul was free to continue in the journey of exploration and understanding. That's how I view it, and

I don't think I'd be this indifferent to death if I wasn't a practicing Witch. We just don't think about it. It's not an ending, but a new beginning."

Paul's solitary lifestyle began in the military, where, he said, most Witches practiced alone and got together mainly to talk about their unique position in a world that seemed to favor conservative denominations. Working alone continued to provide Paul with more time to dedicate to rituals he deemed especially significant. He felt an affinity with the waning phase of the moon because it is the time for banishment and change. Healing magic is sometimes practiced during this period. Often, retreating to his own garden where he grew a multitude of herbs, Paul collected ingredients he would later use to brew tonics, teas or ointments for his patients. Unlike most Witches, he seemed less concerned with psychic phenomena. It was clear to me as we sat at a corner table in a diner in Newport Village that Paul's greatest goals as a Witch had to do with marrying the factual and the esoteric. He catered to a number of private clients as a holistic counselor, instructing them on how to use various herbal medications while delving into meditation, curative visualization or the practice of yoga. On the nights of the full moon, he worshipped the Goddess by lighting candles and incense and writing poetry. He had no altars in his home, nor did he have a designated space used solely for magickal endeavors. Undoubtedly, Paul was perhaps the simplest Witch I had met, and, in a way, his practices seemed to me as more general than centralized. Had he not referred to himself as a Witch, I may have just as well thought him a New Age groupie.

"That's not entirely untrue," he said when confronted with my observation. "But I don't think the Goddess denies me worship because I don't cast circles and chant and dance around with a coven. That's fine for the Witches who do. Wicca is a religion, but to me it's more a way of life. I guess I'm the perfect example as to why the word *Witch* can't really be defined completely. We have different practices, different theories about what works and what doesn't. Mainly, though, we're all drawing from the same energy pool in our quest to live harmonious lives balanced by nature. I do cast spells and perform rituals, but they're few and far between."

He then gave me an example. Several years ago, only two weeks before sitting for his R.N. boards, Paul was standing in the shower when his hand grazed over an unusual lump on the back of his neck. Alarmed, he saw his doctor, who immediately scheduled surgery. The partial diagnosis was of an enlarged lymph gland. It could have been a result of minor infection, but a biopsy was planned. Fearing the worst, Paul set to cure himself "by way of the earth." The moon, then in a waning phase, acted as his guide. He took a human-shaped black candle and marked an X over the neck area. He meditated and employed a banishing ritual to rid his body of whatever ailed it. The Goddess Hecate, an auspicious deity and ruler of the dark side of the moon, was summoned in Roman and Greek times to expel disease. Her trademark is the crossroads. In keeping with the mindset of that Pagan era, Paul walked to a crossroads not far from his home and there scattered the remnants of the black candle.

"I used the darkness to counteract the darkness," he explained. "During the waning cycle of the moon, the human body is depleted of regular energy and more prone to discomfort. Women menstruate more in these two weeks than when the moon is waxing or full, and fewer babies are born. As the gravitational pull decreases in the atmosphere, so do our bodily functions. It's similar to what happens with the ocean tides. I meditated on the natural darkness of this time and used it to balance what was skewed inside me."

In essence, Paul neutralized the negativity in his body. Much like the toxicity levels in the chemotherapy used to treat cancer patients, the energy he harnessed had both good and bad side effects. When he returned to the doctor several days later, a sec-

ond X ray revealed no trace of the swollen lymph gland in his
neck. He kept copies of both X rays. A follow-up battery of tests
performed on him revealed no abnormalities. Though apparently
cured of one ailment, he suffered for several weeks from drain
ing migraines, until the moon went from waxing to full. It was
an example of the body's ability to transcend itself through its
natural surroundings.

"I think one of the problems with Wicca today is the importance practitioners place on their 'powers,'" Paul said. "In their
need to show the public that what we do is real, and that it
works, they unintentionally paint themselves as freaks, or as un-
commonly gifted. That isn't true. Anyone has the potential to be
a Witch. I can't stress enough that so much of Wicca is scientific
because it's based on the idea of Mother Earth."

In the main, Paul asserted, Wicca is a religion that success-
fully conjoins the scientific with the spiritual. The resurgence of
interest in Witches is not, in his opinion, unusual or fleeting.
"What we're seeing so much of today—herbalism, holistic medicine, a return to what's called 'New Age'—is really a return to
the old ways, and to the roots of Paganism. Even angelic inter-
vention seems vaguely Pagan to me. In pre-Christian Europe,
Witches might not have had angels, but they had Familiars.
They had guardians who were considered deities. People all over
America are rethinking their spiritual selves right now. Minds
are opening up. People are connecting more with the earth.
Whether they know it or not, they're connecting with the
Goddess."

Sacred Site

MOUNT KATAHDIN, MAINE

The Abenaki Native Americans have lived on this site and its surrounding areas for nearly ten thousand years. The mount is also sacred to the Penobscot Indians. Both tribes believe that the benevolent spirit residing in its peaks controls weather patterns and ushers in the seasons. For local residents, the site is as majestic as it is magical; many have described Mount Katahdin as brimming with the true essence of nature and the elements. It is a rare corner of America, far removed from the concrete jungles that have consumed our major cities. When walking through the wooded trails, one cannot help but feel an intimate connection to the land. Twilit paths and a placid, nearby lake seem to reflect the rituals of centuries past, when our Native ancestors drew down the rains through dance and drum and deity.

Chapter Five

The Magickal Basics

The person who has never dreamed of casting a spell is a rare person to find. Most of us can remember the exact moment when we first wished for that magickal love potion or secret herb, that lucky incantation or talisman. How disappointing it was to walk away from the initial excitement empty-handed! More disappointing still was the belief that nothing more could have been done to alter the situation positively. Fate had intervened and dealt a nasty blow. Best to get over it and forget, right? Not necessarily.

The desire to create changes in life is natural. We are not born in full armor, ready and able to face the world without a backward glance. If that were the case, we wouldn't focus so much energy on trying to revamp our imperfect little selves. We wouldn't spend inordinate amounts of time imagining what *might* or *could* be. As children, we fantasized about magick in the classical sense and set our budding minds to carpets that flew and cloaks that held the power to make us invisible. We idolized fictional characters—many of them Witches and Wizards—and tried to emulate their incredible powers. Alas, the experiments didn't work. In our later years, as we came to understand the difference between myth and reality, that seed of interest probably dimmed, but it never completely dissolved. Belief in magick—in any aspect of the supernatural—is ingrained in human consciousness. We all want good luck, happy homes, smooth relationships and lucrative careers. We might also need a boost in income or a bit of protection from the universe. The majority of religions shy away from the possibility of creating change in the material world because the laws of dogma and catechism disallow it. Here, God is the source of everything, and only he can grant the answers to your prayers. Wicca embraces a different system of beliefs. Magick is very real to the practicing Witch, and it is used to enrich life and foster spiritual growth.

History tells us that the concept of magick is timeless. Every culture and civilization subscribed to its own system of otherworldly beliefs. Shamans, witch doctors and medicine men have been with us since Paleolithic times, shaping the forces of nature to do their bidding. Many of these ancient practices are still relevant today. But beyond the chants and herbs and incantations lie a deeper meaning and an ageless universal message. We need magick in our lives. Nature is our own sacred space, and its resources are alive within us and around us. Mankind has never relinquished the longing to progress, to persevere and to explore the promises of the unknown. The resurgence of modern-day Witchcraft is a prime example of this quest for knowledge and understanding. In divinity, we find the boundless possibilities of prosperity, knowledge and change. In magick, we find ourselves.

Beginning the Magick: Preparations

No book on Wicca, Witchcraft or Paganism can address the practice of magick without stressing how important it is to *begin slowly*. This does not necessarily refer to the number of spells you cast; much more so it has to do with your rising levels of interest and the excitement you're feeling. Sometimes it can lead you astray. Once you come to understand how to raise energy and cast spells, you'll have the urge to work them almost every night. This might build on the old adage that practice makes perfect, but it will also affect you physically and emotionally. Magick is energy. More precisely, it's *your* energy. It requires a lot of work to gather it, ground it, center it and then manifest it. Not every spell will yield results. You'll have especially sour consequences if you don't take the time to weigh the balance of what you're doing.

First, ask yourself all of the necessary—and rudimentary—questions. Why are you casting this spell or performing this particular magick? Is it for you or someone else? If it is for another person, make certain you don't violate his or her will. Consider the Witch's Rede. Your magick should be for a positive purpose. It should also be clearly defined. Is it? Don't just sit before a candle and say: *Well, now...I really could use some good luck dust sprinkled over every area of my life. And I could use some cold hard cash, too. Yep, that'll do it.* But it will do absolutely nothing. Your magickal focus must be broken down to a very specific goal. You might project for good luck, but how is that luck going to manifest? Picture the exact corner of your life you wish to influence. Direction, here, is a good thing. Don't hold back. The more detailed you are, the better.

So there is the first bit of advice: have a plan.

Now let's talk about this strange thing called magick. Do you understand it? Do you comprehend how it works? Too many beginners read one book on Wicca and think they've got the hang of it. Truth is, it takes a long time to become well versed and fluent in the language of magick. It is not, by any means, simple. When considering magick, remember that it is a natural force. The current you will eventually tap into is flowing around you right now, at this very moment. You will be harnessing it and then shaping it through your own mental powers. Magick begins in the mind. It begins with *you*. Do not go about casting spells if the basic system of magick fails to make sense. The results will be disappointing, as you will probably have no results at all.

A second kernel of Wiccan wisdom: know your stuff.

Once you come full circle in your understanding of magick, you will feel empowered. The universe is listening to you. The world is full of possibility. You will immediately be in sync with nature. Every area of your life will hold the potential for magick and you just might start changing things for the better. But hold tight to one rule: do not brag about being a Witch to other people. Never discuss your magick with those who know nothing of how Witchcraft works. Too often, the curiosity of others comes at a high price, and you don't want their negative thoughts and opinions floating around. Keep your spells confined to your own altar or—at the most—with another practitioner who will recognize and appreciate the process. The urge to speak out in favor of your religious beliefs is tempting, but stay clear of it. Wisdom is silent.

Ground and Center

Energy is like blood: it flows in unison with the rhythms of the body. Learning how to ground and center your energy before performing magick is essential. This will keep the current flowing smoothly. Visualization techniques work best here. Eventually, you will create your own methods for grounding and centering, but the following technique works nicely.

Stand straight in the center of the floor, your arms at your sides. (If you are outside, on a patch of grass, all the better. If not, make certain the room you are using is free of clutter.) Plant your feet firmly on the ground. Close your eyes and breathe deeply. Imagine a white energy light flowing upward from deep within the earth. It courses into your feet, your toes, your ankles. It rises slowly up your legs. Feel the pulse of it as it radiates farther up along the length of your body. Your heart is feeling it too, beating a bit faster. Continue breathing deeply but do not lose sight of the white light. See it pouring over your face, your eyes and finally your head. In your mind's eye, you are beaming and pulsating with energy, blotted out by it. Pull it up from the earth and let it fill you.

Exhale slowly.

Little by little, begin relinquishing the energy. Imagine it receding, dropping away from your head and face, sinking down past your neck. As it passes each point on your body, feel the coolness of the air around you. You might also feel your heart slowing down a bit. Let the energy fall out of you and back into the earth. Picture the white light branching out into a number of small, strong lines as it leaves your feet. The lines are like roots, digging and pushing through the soil in their struggle to go deeper. See the lines descending farther into the earth. Within a few minutes, they should be completely submerged.

Remain standing with your eyes closed. The light has returned to its source, but the power flooded your body fully and left its imprint. Envision yourself as a sparkling orb, twinkling with a series of diamond points. The energy is flowing through you now: it has been raised and grounded. You will center it when you perform your next magickal endeavor.

Sacred Space

Creating sacred space is an important part of every Witch's life and magick. In your home or apartment, you might have already set aside a corner for your altar or ritual tools; maybe a square of your kitchen counter is sectioned off for herbs. Location is not important so long as you understand the meaning behind sacred space. This is the dwelling where you become one with your spirituality, where your subconscious mind opens up to new journeys. The sacred space is consecrated and ritually charged and must be kept free of dust, dirt and any debris. It is not uncommon to walk into a Witch's home and find an elaborately decorated altar or tabletop. He or she might not be performing magick any time soon, but the space serves as a reminder to her that she is always walking on precious, hallowed ground.

If you have not created your own sacred space, go about doing it now. Don't worry if your living quarters are cramped—the slightest corner or patch of floor can act as your guide. First, you will want to clean the chosen area. Then prepare a mixture of salt, water and a bit of your favorite scented oil. Sprinkle the mixture over and around your space while you gently invoke the elements. Summon water and air to purify. Call fire to burn away the imprint of unwanted energies. Let earth come in to ground and center your own desire for positive action. If at all possible, place a charm or some sort of special object over the area. If not, just remember to respect the space by keeping it clean. Meditate in it daily. Read the Tarot or write your own spells there. The idea is to infuse the sacred space with your essence.

The casting of the magick circle is the creation of sacred space, but here, the space is done and undone often within an hour or two. It is more *charged* than *consecrated*. It is also a place of protection. In time, you will come to understand that sacred space can be made your own just about anywhere—inside or outside, in hotel rooms or dormitories, in country backyards or city gardens. You have to know only the boundaries of your space, where it begins and ends.

The Pennsylvania Dutch: Powwowing Magick

The powwowers of the Pennsylvania Dutch were consulted to cure a number of physical ailments, from warts and hemorrhaging to certain types of cancers. The powwower would chant a series of words such as the Christian Apostles' Creed over a patient and perhaps instruct him or her to perform an act three times. Ill children, for example, were "passed through" the legs of a table (or crawled underneath it) three times to ensure completion of a cure. Oftentimes, charms were employed to rid one of disease or bad luck, as was the use of strings and object transference. Powwowers also had a reputation for specializing in their cures: Some were successful at treating bruises and burns while others eased the pains of broken bones and maladies of the skin. Powwowing always partakes of chant, voice and prayer.

In the seventeenth and eighteenth centuries, powwowers were consulted regularly in Pennsylvania Dutch society. They did not request payment for their services but accepted gifts and offerings as signs of gratitude. The specific chants and prayers of powwowing were passed on through familial lineage, but in what the Dutch called "crossways"—from male to female and vice versa. There was no distinct identity attributed to the powwower. One could be male or female, old or young, a housewife, farmer or local businessman. The Protestant faith shunned powwowing, however, and branded it evil; nevertheless, though many powwowers did their business underground, the practice is alive and well today.

Jennifer M., a homemaker in Connecticut, was born in Pennsylvania and grew up with a powwowing grandfather. When I contacted her for an interview, she admitted that she rarely discussed her powwowing lineage for fear of ridicule.

"My family is very big, and we grew up knowing that when we got a fever or felt sick, our grandfather would probably be able to cure us," she explained. "I never thought of powwowing as Witchcraft, but it's definitely a form of folk magick. You don't really learn the truth of it through books or television shows. It's an all-in-the-family kind of thing."

When asked to describe a particular powwowing practice or ritual, Jennifer explained the idea behind object transference. "When my brother was ten he developed a cyst on his ankle," she said. "My grandfather, who spoke German fluently, bent down and chanted loudly over my brother's ankle. He then made my brother walk through the doorway of the house three times. After that, my grandfather rubbed a mixture of herbs on the cyst. The idea was to draw the disease out of my brother's body and into the herbs. The disease was then transferred and removed. I was fifteen at the time and remember everything about it. It worked."

Powwowing has become popular among many American Witches because it is directly linked to healing, herbalism and chanting. It was not at all difficult to find practitioners who employ various powwowing techniques in their rituals and spells. One was Michael J., a high priest of Wicca, who runs his own coven in a suburb of Boston.

"The great thing about powwowing is its versatility," he explained. "It's an intimate form of folk magick but it's also very wide-ranging. You can use it for healing people or animals, and you can also use it for agricultural purposes. The Pennsylvania Dutch used it to help their crops grow. It requires a Witch to learn the secrets of voice and hand gestures. There isn't necessarily a need for spellwork or ritual with it. You just have to know, through proper training, how and where to direct the energy."

The efficacy of powwowing cannot be disputed. It originated with German emigrants but was practiced widely on American soil. Once an esoteric tradition, it is today growing in scope and popularity among practitioners of Wicca and folk magick.

American Witch

SILVER RAVENWOLF

A prolific and popular writer of books on Wicca, Silver RavenWolf has an international reputation as a spokesperson for the Pagan and Wiccan communities. Her work has explored virtually every corner of modern-day Witchcraft, from folk magick and prosperity spells to angels and herbalism. She is a Wiccan priestess and professional astrologer. Her initiated lineage includes ties to Gerald Gardner.

RavenWolf found national acclaim upon the publication of her first book, *To Ride a Silver Broomstick*, in 1990. She has since produced eighteen subsequent volumes. One of her most popular, *Teen Witch,* spawned a phenomenon among younger readers. She is active on the publicity circuit and has appeared on television, radio and in countless magazines and newspapers. RavenWolf travels around the country lecturing about her work and the positive aspects of her religion. A special interest of RavenWolf's is the "Powwow" magick indigenous to the German settlers of rural Pennsylvania, in which she was formally trained. She served as director of the Wiccan/Pagan Press Alliance for over fifteen years.

Currently, RavenWolf is director of the Black Forest Clan, comprised of Witches from various social and ethnic backgrounds. As the second highest-selling author at Llewellyn Publications, her appeal to today's American Witch is enormous.

www.silverravenwolf.com

Color Correspondences in Magick

Colors are important in magick. Each represents a different emotion, goal, dream, wish and desire. This very basic list is meant to guide you when performing candle magick.

White: Purification, cleansing, lunar meditations, peace, serenity, spells and rituals honoring the Goddess.

Red: Vitality, passion, courage, all spells and rituals involving love and sex magick

Orange: Spells and rituals honoring the God, the sun and solar deities; loyalty, hope and aggression

Yellow: Personal development, confidence, intellect and communication

Green: Luck, prosperity, all spells and rituals honoring nature

Pink: Love and friendship, healing, compassion

Brown: Emotional security, spells for the home, safety

Silver: Intuition, psychic awareness, astral travel

Purple: Healing, change, banishing negativity, spells and rituals involving revolution or rebirth

Blue: Meditation and intelligence, communication, spells for career

Black: Protection, to neutralize harm and negativity, to counteract ill will

Herbal and Botanical Magick

The use of herbs in magick, ritual and healing is significant to the practice of modern-day Witchcraft. Herbs possess a multitude of medicinal properties and they also remind us of our eternal connection to nature. They are a part of the circle of being every Witch honors. Tonics, brews and the occasional potion have been around since the dawn of time. In pre-Christian Europe, every small village or town had its resident midwife who knew which plants healed disease and which protected people against harm. These traditions are alive and well today.

When you're using herbs, it is of utmost importance to do so in an educated fashion. Too much of a certain ingredient can be harmful, and too little will produce no results at all. You may harness the power of herbs for divination or to cast a spell. In some instances, they might provide fragrance for a ritual bath. Whatever the case, you will need to know the names of herbs and their magickal intentions. This list is not exhaustive but it will provide you with a basic understanding of herbalism. Consult the directory at the back of this book to find occult supply shops closest to you for further information.

- *Acacia:* Traditionally, this wood is burned for prosperity, or to attract money. It is also a common ingredient used to try to enhance psychic phenomena. For divination, burn it on an eve of the full moon.

- *Allspice:* Also used for luck-related magick, these berries can be crushed into a powder and added to a basic candle spell. For healing, the powder is sprinkled into a colored flannel pouch and worn.

- *Aloe:* Commonly used for healing purposes where bruises, burns and cuts are concerned, aloe is also a pow-

erful protector. Deposit a piece in the glove compartment of your car, or hang in your home to ward off negativity.

- *Angelica:* A powerful agent to dispel bad vibes, remove
  curses and protect, angelica is also used in spirit communication and to enhance prophetic dreaming.

- *Aniseeds:* These aromatic seeds provide a sense of calm
  and well-being for any ritual. They are also used to aid
  in meditation and past-life regression.

- *Balm of Gilead:* When love is in the air, use this potent
  flower for spells or rituals that involve sex magick, attraction, desire and any other matter of the heart. It is
  also believed to bring a sense of tranquillity and calm.

- *Basil:* In addition to its wonderful flavor, basil is associated with wealth, luck and love. Crush the leaves and add
  them to a new moon incantation for prosperity. When
  the moon is waning, charge the leaves and wear them for
  protection.

- *Bay Laurel:* Burning these leaves, which are frequently
  used in divination or while scrying, can also cleanse a
  room of negative feelings or past influences. Bay laurel
  serves well for banishing rituals.

- *Bergamot:* Gamblers often add these leaves or roots to
  their wallets because bergamot is believed to attract money
  and good luck. Its fortunate properties are used in healing magick.

- *Birch:* The wood of the birch tree has long been used in
  sacred rites and ceremonies. It is best burned for protection and the warding off of negativity.

- *Bistort:* This herb is frequently used in fertility magick or
  to aid couples and lovers in sex magick. When mixed
  with other herbs, it can heighten psychic phenomena.

- *Burdock:* When hung in the home, burdock is believed to bring happiness and a general sense of contentment. When worn in a flannel pouch, it aids in protection.

- *Caraway:* These seeds grant protection when worn, and if used in ritual can have positive results on the mind.

- *Carnation:* The petals of the carnation can spark energy and zest. They are also known for aiding in matters related to creativity and artistic endeavor. In healing magick, add petals to fresh water or burn on the eve of the full moon.

- *Celandine:* When worn as an amulet or made into a charm, this herb brings peace of mind and is believed to attract spiritual guardians to your side.

- *Celery Seeds:* These are most often used as an ingredient in sex magick or love spells. It has been said that carrying celery seeds will attract passion into your life.

- *Chamomile:* When drunk as a tea, chamomile provides relaxation, serenity and peace. It is used in healing to calm disorders of the nervous system. Place two lukewarm tea bags upon the eyes for inflammation or infection.

- *Cinnamon:* In addition to its sweetness, cinnamon brings luck and prosperity to those who employ it in magick. Sprinkle a pinch of it into your wallet, beside your bank book or inside a cash register to keep finances on the rise.

- *Cinquefoil:* Sacred to Jupiter, the planet of luck, this herb acts as a receptor to all things fortunate. Thus, it is employed in spells and rituals that involve love, prosperity, justice, marriage, physical changes and emotional stability. For healing, burn crushed remnants on the night of the full moon.

- *Cloves:* Used often for protection, or to neutralize negativity. When cloves are tied together and strung over a doorway, they are believed to bring harmony and mental calm.

- *Coriander:* This herb is most commonly used in fertility magick and in love spells. Because of its affiliation to water it is also associated with emotions and dreams.

- *Damiana:* According to legend, this herb is an aphrodisiac and should be employed in any workings of sex magick or love spells.

- *Dandelion:* When drunk as a tea, dandelion promotes healing and physical regeneration. Perform a banishing ritual on an eve of the waning moon and burn dandelion for protection. On an eve of the waxing moon, use it to communicate with the spirit realm.

- *Dill:* Dill has long been believed to provide extraordinary protection where infants and children are concerned. Hanging a bit of it over a nursery or any other doorway will bring security and foster safety. When the moon is waxing and in Venus, burn a bit of dill to enhance a love spell.

- *Dittany of Crete:* Burn these dried leaves to foster trance channeling or mediumistic skills. Its astral properties are believed to enhance transcendent mental experiences.

- *Dragon's Blood:* Traditionally, a small resin of dragon's blood packs quite a punch to ward off negativity and neutralize harmful forces. It can be ingested in small amounts, most commonly in red wine.

- *Eucalyptus:* The leaves of the eucalyptus tree are an excellent source of healing, most notably for ailments of the nose, throat and sinuses. When worn or hung in the home, it is believed to keep illnesses at bay.

- *Eyebright:* Psychic abilities are frequently intensified when this herb is employed in magick and ritual. Its reference to vision implies clairvoyance and extrasensory perception.

- *Fennel:* Fennel has long been a protective herb, and traditionally it is known to rebuff evil or unruly spirits. Employ it in Samhain rituals, or when performing banishing rituals in the waning phase of the moon.

- *Fenugreek:* Adding fenugreek to money and prosperity spells enhances results. It is known for its luck-drawing properties.

- *Fern:* Burning sprigs of fern will heighten mental stimulation and aid in concentration. As an incense, it can provide a sense of calm and tranquillity.

- *Gardenia:* The gardenia flower is a bearer of peace and accord. Burning petals will soften the edges of a bad breakup or troubled friendship.

- *Garlic:* This herb has a history of protecting those who wear it as an amulet or hang it in their homes. It is also useful in binding and banishing rituals. Those in need of a willpower boost should employ it when casting spells for self-growth or change.

- *Gingerroot:* In many Eastern superstitions, gingerroot is believed to bring power and influence to those who wear it on their person. In magick, it can be burned to ensure success in all ventures.

- *Ginseng:* To promote an attractive self-image and beauty, use ginseng in self-initiation rites. It should also be employed for healing magick and love spells.

- *Hawthorn:* Burning remnants of this wood aids in career matters. It is also a good source for spells involving court cases or legal matters.

- *Heather:* Hang this herb when performing healing rituals. It is often used for purification and to promote self-growth.

- *Holly:* Lure and legend tell us that holly was hung in homes to ward off negativity and to promote protection. It should also be placed on an altar during winter solstice rituals.

- *Honeysuckle:* In addition to enhancing love rituals, honeysuckle is an excellent agent to stimulate psychic awareness. For prosperity, it should be burned with a basic candle spell.

- *Hyacinth:* Carry hyacinth on your person to bring protection and to neutralize negativity. For magickal purposes, employ it during fertility rituals, as it is believed to foster conception.

- *Hyssop:* This herb produces wonderful results in spells and rituals relating to prosperity and luck. Burn it with an incantation to Jupiter.

- *Irish Moss:* Use in all matters relating to money and finances. When the moon is waxing, cast a spell for luck and place some Irish moss on your altar.

- *Ivy:* According to some ancient legends, ivy was grown along the outside walls of homes because it repelled evil spirits. It still possesses the same protective properties. It is also useful in love spells.

- *Jasmine:* The flowers of jasmine are excellent for love rituals. They are also believed to enhance prophetic dreams.

- *Juniper:* When the moon is waning, use juniper in any banishing rituals. It can be used as well for love spells or sex magick. Its healing properties can enhance rituals for ailments of the nose and throat.

- *Lavender:* Burn lavender petals for purification, especially when moving into a new home or apartment. Lavender is also useful in self-dedication rites.

- *Marigold:* Marigold has been used to promote peace and serenity, especially for newlyweds. Associated with Venus, it is also burned for matters relating to love and passion.

- *Marjoram:* Employ marjoram when scrying or in any rituals involving divination. It is especially powerful when honoring the Goddess and God because of its abilities to bring about balance and harmony.

- *Mint:* An excellent source of healing. Mint can be drunk as a tea to aid in digestion or burned in healing rituals. Carrying mint is believed to keep one away from potentially dangerous situations.

- *Mistletoe:* Hung in the home, usually over a doorway, mistletoe keeps negative influences at bay. When worn, it is said to aid in protection.

- *Mugwort:* This versatile herb can be used in spells and rituals that involve strength, courage and protection. It is believed to stimulate psychic energy and clairvoyance, as well as astral travel. Burn on the full moon for maximum results.

- *Mustard:* Adding seeds to money rituals will bring especially positive results. Mustard also enhances intellect and emotional balance.

- *Myrrh:* It was once believed that myrrh attracted the help of various nature spirits. It is therefore beneficial to use when gardening or planting new trees. In magick and ritual, myrrh aids in meditation.

- *Nettle:* Burn nettle leaves for protection, or when performing banishing rituals. It is also useful in healing magick, especially to ease disorders of the nervous system.

- *Nutmeg:* Use nutmeg in prosperity rituals, either to anoint candles or as an altar decoration. It can also be employed for divination and to enhance psychic abilities. Carrying nutmeg stimulates confidence.

- *Oak:* This most sacred wood has many useful purposes. Burn it to promote a strong sense of self-image or courage, or to magnify patience. It also stimulates mental activity and intelligence.

- *Onion:* When buried beside a house, an onion will dispel bad luck. Its cleansing properties are useful in banishing rituals, or when casting spells to break bad habits or end negative relationships.

- *Orris:* On a night when the moon is waxing and in the astrological sign of Taurus, burn orris for love or to attract a mate into your life. Sprinkle remnants over a picture of your beloved to ensure faithfulness.

- *Parsley:* Burning parsley, which is often used in fertility rituals, will bring about abundance. It also cleanses, and so it should be used in magick and rituals that involve purification. Rubbing parsley over an infected area of the body will promote healing.

- *Pennyroyal:* Pennyroyal is frequently used in self-initiation rites. It stimulates psychic activity and clairvoyance. When burned, pennyroyal aids in protection.

- *Peppermint:* Any purification rituals should involve peppermint. Burning it will cleanse the immediate atmosphere of negativity. For love rituals, peppermint brings about swift results.

- *Rose:* Traditionally, the rose was believed to produce feelings of love and attraction. It is still a powerful ingredi-

ent in love and sex magick. Spells involving beauty or
self-image should employ rose petals.

- *Rue:* An excellent source of protection. Placing a bit of
rue in your home, office or car will parry negative influences. When worn, it is believed to promote healing and
a general sense of well-being.

- *Sage:* Sage is a common ingredient in healing magick
and rituals for balance and emotional serenity. It can also
be used in money spells, or for prosperity.

- *St. John's Wort:* This herb has long been used to cure ailments of the nervous system, and to bring about feelings
of peace. Make it into an amulet and wear it for protection.

- *Skullcap:* When burned, this herb aids in meditation and
deep trance states. It is believed to promote a sense of
calm in the mind and body.

- *Solomon's Seal:* As an incense, this herb wards off negativity. It was once believed to parry attacks from evil spirits.
It should be used for purification rituals, and to banish
unwanted habits or unhealthy relationships

- *Thyme:* Especially useful in dream magick, thyme promotes astral travel and keeps nightmares at bay. Burn it
during love rituals, or as an incense for sex magick.

- *Tonka Beans:* For business owners, tonka beans will attract money when deposited in a cash register. Place
them around jars of loose change as well. They should
be employed in prosperity and luck rituals, or when casting spells for leadership and power.

- *Vervain:* Create an amulet with vervain to keep negativity at bay. It also aids in purification rituals and love magick. Keeping some vervain in a sealed pouch is believed
to inspire creativity.

- *Vetivert:* Vetivert is a common ingredient in luck spells. Adding vetivert to an altar during a candle spell is believed to attract the spirits of good fortune.

- *Violets:* Burning petals of the violet flower will aid in love magick. Wearing them on your person will bring luck. To attract a special someone, place dried violets under your pillow and meditate upon them before sleep.

- *Willow:* Burn willow wood in divination rituals, or to enhance prophetic dreams. In healing magick, willow fights against ailments of the chest. Wearing it aids in protection.

- *Witch Hazel:* An excellent ingredient for healing ailments of the face and skin, witch hazel is also useful for purification and cleansing.

Mineral Magick: Stones of the Earth

Mineral magick is one of the simplest and easiest ways to heighten spells and rituals. Very little preparation is needed. You gather your stones or minerals the day before casting a spell or performing a ritual, deposit them in a glass jar and remove them when you are building your altar. They can be used for decorative purposes or as points of concentration when meditating. It is the corresponding energy of the particular stones or minerals that will aid you in your magick.

- *Agate:* A powerful stone, agate stimulates the mind. It aids the senses and brings tranquillity. One should be carried for protection, or to promote good health.

- *Alexandrite:* Very useful for ailments of the nervous system, alexandrite has strong healing properties and can be employed as an altar decoration when casting spells for self-growth, knowledge and empowerment.

- *Amazonite:* This stone has a strong influence on the chakras. It is also believed to strengthen one's faith in any area of life. Carry it to promote courage in difficult times.

- *Amber:* Often used in love spells and rituals, amber is a popular Witch's tool. It promotes attraction and desire.

- *Amethyst:* It is believed that an amethyst can increase psychic abilities and communication with the spirit world. Many Witches use the amethyst when reading the tarot or holding séances.

- *Apache Tears:* This stone brings out one's analytical nature, and should be carried where business and financial matters are concerned.

- *Apatite:* A tool for the mind, apatite increases intelligence and emotional balance. It is believed that holding it will cure one of a headache or migraine.

- *Aquamarine:* A protective stone, aquamarine is known for keeping dangerous situations at bay. It also enhances psychic awareness.

- *Aventurine:* Long considered a lucky stone, aventurine attracts money and prosperity and should be carried by gamblers. In healing magick, it works wonders on diseases of the eyes.

- *Azurite:* This stone is excellent for raising energy. It should be employed in all rituals and spells because it will ground one for meditation and then stimulate a magickal current.

- *Black Obsidian:* An excellent stone for divination or scrying, black obsidian should be worn to avoid obstacles and remove blockages.

- *Bloodstone:* Bloodstone creates alignment in the body and promotes physical awareness. In magick and ritual, it can be used to counteract low energy or other ailments of the body.

- *Calcite:* Calcite's numerous magickal properties can be used in healing magick for ailments of the kidneys and blood. It is also carried by those afflicted with diseases of the bones.

- *Carnelian:* When placed in the home, carnelian acts to repel negative influences and illness. When carried, it stimulates creativity.

- *Celestite:* Carry this stone when stress levels are at their high point. It relieves nervous tension and simultaneously promotes serenity. It can also be used in magick and ritual to heighten clairvoyance.

- *Citrine*: Citrine aids in protection and should be used in banishing rituals. It is also believed to affect the solar plexus.

- *Clear Quartz:* The mind is awakened to the powers of the clear quartz. Energy levels peak. Intelligence and balance are aligned. When carried, it promotes courage and assuages fear.

- *Coral:* Associated with the sun, coral has a long and magickal history. It brings warmth into a home. It provides protection and heightens the senses. It is also considered a luck magnet and a powerful tool in love spells.

- *Crocoite:* A healing stone, crocoite aids in ailments of the torso and chest, and the internal organs. Carry it to bring about energy and vitality.

- *Diamond:* Rare and coveted, the diamond is more than just a girl's best friend. Among its many magickal properties, it brings protection and keeps negativity at bay, repels disease and nurtures power.

- *Emerald:* Also very rare, an emerald is the proverbial love stone. It attracts desire and is said to create harmony between two people. When worn or carried, it also provides protection.

- *Garnet:* Legend has it that a garnet will keep a marriage strong. It promotes union and emotional balance.

- *Hematite:* Hematite aids in healing magick for ailments of the blood. It can help raise energy in ritual, and it also brings about feelings of peace and serenity.

- *Jasper:* Used in healing rituals for ailments of the nervous system, jasper, when carried, gives off a soothing energy. In magick and ritual, it is a passport for astral travel.

- *Kunzite:* Hold this stone when meditating. It can be used to ground and center before casting spells or performing rituals. A popular belief is that kunzite strengthens confidence.

- *Lapis Lazuli:* According to legend and folklore, lapis lazuli heightens psychic energy and aids in clairvoyance. It also creates balance. In magick and ritual, it should be used to connect with deity or for spirit communication.

- *Moonstone:* The moonstone is mystical. Carrying it will bring protection and holding it in the palm of your hand will ease stress and tension. Meditate upon the moonstone when performing rituals for ailments of the blood or female reproductive system.

- *Peridot:* Useful in raising energy, especially for love

spells, peridot is also believed to aid ailments of the digestive system.

- *Pyrite:* Use pyrite in banishing rituals or to break bad habits. It has strong protective capabilities.

- *Rhodochrosite:* Depositing rhodochrosite in any corner of your home will keep negativity at bay. Carrying it on your person will grant courage in trying situations.

- *Rose Quartz:* Rose quartz's connection to love magick is very strong. It promotes emotional balance and security and is also used to mend the pangs of a severed relationship.

- *Sodalite:* Use sodalite in full moon rituals to enhance community and union with the Gods. It possesses strong universal energies that can affect emotions positively.

- *Sunstone:* Use sunstone when Drawing Down the Sun, or in rituals that honor the Horned God. It is also believed to bring luck to anyone who carries it.

- *Turquoise:* Turquoise is best if used for purification rituals, to cleanse the aura and remove negativity. It also aids in protection. According to legend and folklore, those who carry or wear the turquoise stone will avert danger.

Bewitchin' Sex: From Spells to Spanking

To the modern Witch or Pagan, sex is revered and celebrated as the physical union between consenting adults. Acts of love and pleasure are rituals sacred to the Gods because they remind us of the intimate power inherent in our own bodies. The union between male and female brings forth the miracle of life, but it also heightens the senses and invigorates the mind. Wicca does not view sex as sinful or gluttonous – it simply welcomes it. There is nothing hedonistic in this belief. When we are honest with our true selves, we come to realize that sex is a basic human need. It is as much a corporeal odyssey as it is a spiritual one. Mining our own desires and fantasies is akin to letting go of fear, shame and untapped curiosity. When practiced responsibly and harmlessly, sexual exploration brings us to a place that is altogether natural. And it is in nature that Wicca resides.

One of the most interesting practitioners I met while researching *American Witch* was a woman named Rosslynne. A Wiccan priestess since 1992, Ross belonged to a New York City–based coven for three years before branching out into solitary practice. The decision was motivated by her desire to concentrate her energies on sex magick and "the melding of self and spirit through ecstasy."

"I've always been a very sexual person," Ross explained. "When I was in my twenties, I had a number of wonderful relationships, but because I was raised in a Christian home, I always felt like I was doing something wrong and unethical. But the truth is that I felt most connected to a higher power while having sex. Not to sound clichéd, but it really was the meaning of ecstasy to me. It was the closest I ever got to exploring my own femininity."

Ross grew curious about feminine spirituality and began attending Goddess-oriented workshops in New York and Massachusetts. Wicca, she said, was the religion she had always dreamed of, but until that time she hadn't much knowledge of the Pagan movement. When she joined a coven, she was introduced to ritual and spell-casting. She also felt connected to a "siblinghood" of like-minded people who understood her views about sex and sexual exploration. It was the ritual aspect of Wicca, however, that truly stuck a chord within her.

"The coven I was a member of was largely Alexandrian, and

we performed most of our rituals skyclad [naked]," Ross said. "It's an incredibly freeing experience. I realized that I was able to let everything go and get to the root of my true physical self, and that led me deeper into my subconscious and to spirituality. As a Witch, I feel like it's my responsibility to experience and learn as much as I can in this world, and I know how powerful sexual experiences can be. That's my own personal take on magick – the sexual kind is what opens doors to all levels of consciousness."

Today, Ross is a solitary Witch and a professional dominatrix. Her New York apartment is home to a "select" group of clients, all of whom have experienced her unique blend of sex and modern magick. Ross explained that as a dominatrix, she does not engage in intercourse with her clients but partakes of their sexual fantasies in an abstract way. She uses traditional magickal techniques—herbalism, chakra energy and meditation, for example—to help them achieve gratification. She does not see herself as a Wiccan spokesperson.

"If a client comes to me with a specific fantasy or request, I begin by asking him or her why they want it and what they hope to experience from it," Ross explained. "And truthfully, people who come to me aren't interested in intercourse – they've already done that and could probably go and get it anywhere. They come to me because they want to transcend the ordinary sexual realm. This can be anything from bondage to massage. They want that ultimate mind-blowing spiritual experience, something that will make them say, 'Oh, wow. I didn't know I could feel that way. I didn't know I was capable of feeling that.' At the beginning of a session, I start out with meditation and bring the client into a very relaxed state. I light candles and incense. To me it's a ritual experience, and I never forget while I'm doing it that I'm a Witch."

I asked Ross to provide me with an example of how magick helps her work. Did her clients ever mind that she was a Witch?

"If a client comes to me and says he wants to know more

about the magickal side of sex, and this a fairly common request, I might brew a tea of chamomile and orange peel to relax him, and then I'll mix a bit of honey with ground peppermint and apply a dab of it to the base of his spine and just below his navel," she said. "The mixture is stimulating, and it can tingle in all the right places. But before beginning a session, I've already prepared a client psychologically through meditation and visualization. I help them open up their chakras for better energy flow and connect with their inner instincts."

Ross explained the process further and said one of the most amazing aspects of her work is observing the aftermath of a client's satisfaction. Some pant and laugh. Others cry because of the intensity of the experience. She spoke of men who, before employing her services, knew sex as narrow and routine but came to understand it as limitless and diversified. She also mentioned women who came to know their own sexuality better.

Ross's practice of sex magick involves ritual bondage, light flogging and spanking, and occasional role-playing. The absence of intercourse, she said, is intrinsic to her work because the point of it all is to get people to know themselves and their own bodies better.

"That's another big part of sex magick," Ross told me. "We know that sex releases endorphins in the mind, and that ecstatic state is like a drug in itself. Most people don't pay attention to the current of those moments that build up to climax. It's a cone of power. The orgasmic energy is the most powerful and pure energy our bodies release. I teach my clients to *experience* it, not to simply let it happen. I can do this because I've experienced it myself, and I've experienced it because I'm a Witch."

Despite her somewhat taboo profession, Ross frequently offers advice and instruction to others on sex magick and how to use Wiccan spirituality to enhance lovemaking.

"It's important for anyone and everyone to remember that good sex is about pushing the boundaries," she said. "In order to do that, you have to forget the feelings of guilt or shame. You're never too old to experience sexual ecstasy. I often tell couples to honor the Goddess and God in their lovemaking, and to study their astrological similarities. Gemini rules the shoulders and arms, so if your mate is a Gemini, you might want to start with a massage. There are also certain colors and deities that are best used and invoked on specific days. Creating the right atmosphere can enhance sex magick greatly. It's all about how far you want to go and how intense you want the experience to be."

To Heighten Psychic Power

This is a simple but highly effective method to help in the development of psychic ability. It is important to remember that all magickal workings should be preceded by a calm and confident sense of self. In essence, you must believe in the power before you even begin honing it. Start out by educating yourself on the psychic realm. What is it all about? How do you plan on using your abilities? How deep do you want to go? Many Witches and Pagans seek to improve their mental concentration skills without focusing on ESP or clairvoyance. Others want to blow open the doorways to complete mental power, which may include psychokinesis—the ability to influence matter, as in moving objects or the bending of metal without the benefit of the hands. Either will require a great deal of effort, but begin with the following exercise.

In a quiet room, light a single candle and sit before it. Let your eyes follow the flame's dance for at least one full minute. When you are relaxed, close your eyes and envision your head being encircled by a white light. See it intensify. Feel its pulse and vibrations. Imagine the light drawing in the elements and the forces of nature. Let the circle shrink until it seeps into your skull. Then picture the inner mechanics of your mind: see it as a sort of labyrinth winding through the bright light. Designate a place within the maze where your psychic current resides. Picture it in any way that suits you. It may be a door or a hall, a garden or path. What matters is that you see the image and its positioning very clearly.

Once this is done, channel the white light into the image. Let it spin through and manifest like a vortex. It may take a while— the longer the better. You must become one with the image and the light. Again, it is important to feel the current pulsing in your mind, as vibrant and animate as electricity. Let it manifest. This is the seed of your psychic development, and it will grow over time. Repeat the process as often as possible until you notice a change in your own energy.

Communicating with the Deity

There is no better way to honor the Goddess and God than through ritual. Covens have the added advantage of more stylized practices, but ritual can be just as elaborate and meaningful for the solitary practitioner. It all depends on what you decide to bring to the altar. For a full moon *esbat*, you may want nothing more than a single candle. For Samhain eve, you might light a dozen votives. Every Witch is free to design his or her own system of worship.

In truth, the theatrics of a ritual are not what matter. What is truly important is how you feel before, during and after the ritual. Was it a magickal experience? Did you connect with a particular deity? Is there an electrical charge pulsating through you? Again, as with magick, the accoutrements you acquire are tools; no amount of specific herb or scented oil will bring you to a pure, altered state of consciousness. It is your energy and passion that must surpass the boundaries of the ordinary. This is what it means to communicate with deity.

A powerful ritual will have influence over the mind and the body, so that the subconscious and the physical both know the imprint of transcendence. A Witch friend of mine once told me that in the midst of a successful ritual, he forgot that there would even be an ending: every part of him was wrapped up in communication. Afterward, he longed to return to the beauty and sanctity of the magick circle because the trappings of the day were simply too mundane to accept. The Goddess and God had clearly been present at this particular ritual. When the essence of divinity seeps into your own rituals and magickal workings, you will undoubtedly know it. The process is not subject to time limits, however. It must happen naturally.

The more you create and partake of rituals, the closer you will get to that golden core of knowledge. Rituals attune our minds and bodies to the rhythms of the universe and the patterns of the seasons. We see this when we turn the Wheel of the Year. Every ritual is a celebration of life, death and rebirth. The divine spark within nature does not end, and neither does a Witch's thirst to experience this bounty.

Talk to the Goddess and God. Express yourself through voice, word and song. Rituals build the bridge to transformation.

The Ritual Bath

Cleanliness of the mind and body are essential to all magickal workings. The ritual bath is thus an excellent way to begin your preparations.

Make certain you have chosen any herbs, minerals or stones to be used in the bath beforehand. The experience should be a relaxing but invigorating one, so select more fragrant ingredients if pungency does the trick for you—lavender, rose petals, basil. Of course, you may simply want to run water purely, with only the added benefit of some cleansing sea salt. It is always a wise idea to meditate lightly while taking the ritual bath.

Keep in mind the purpose here, as it is not an ordinary, everyday thing. The magick begins because of your frame of mind. From the moment you step into the water, forces are churning. Your subconscious is working and preparing your senses.

Once inside the bath, think about the magick you will be performing later on. Let the water soothe you. Relinquish any worries or concerns that were biting at you earlier in the day. There is no place for negativity in the ritual bath. In fact, visualize any bad vibes, thoughts or feelings coming off of you and slithering down the drain as you bathe. This assures that you will be cleansed mentally and physically.

A Lunar Meditation Ritual

This ritual can be performed by those already advanced in the ways of Wicca or anyone who wishes to experience the positive energies of the moon. You will need few tools. The point of this ritual is to awaken your senses to a very basic—and very real—aspect of nature.

On a night of the full moon, retire to a quiet and comfortable corner of your home. Find the astrological correspondence to which the moon phase relates and do a bit of reading on it. Regardless of our individual birth signs, we all share similar personality traits and characteristics. Our bodies ultimately function on the same level. Are you an ambitious Leo with a rather introverted side? Do your Scorpio tendencies lack a bit of passion?

On this night, find the astrological sign the full moon is in and think deeply about its various counterparts. Undoubtedly, there will be certain key points that relate to your own personal life—mentally, emotionally or physically. Take a pen and paper and begin listing what you seek from the conjoined energies of the full moon and its corresponding sign. (For example: Capricorn for a career boost or change, Taurus for financial gain, Aquarius for ailments of the blood.) Holding the list in your hands, meditate upon your desires for at least a half hour, thinking of how those changes will impact your daily life for the better.

When you are fully relaxed, close your eyes and visualize the full moon: its brightness, its long rays pulling and letting go of the tides, its white light enveloping you. Manifest your will. Speak to the energies. Later, burn the piece of paper and scatter the ashes in the night wind.

The Rituals

The Rite of Self-Dedication

On a night of the full moon, gather together two white candles, incense, sage and a cup of water sprinkled with salt. Arrange the items on your altar. If at all possible, sit close to a window, as you will draw your inspiration from the moon's light. You may, however, let the candles' flames symbolize the lunar radiance.

Begin by grounding and centering your energy. Light the candles. Spend some time thinking about the imminent ritual. It has arrived after much thought, study and speculation. Before, you might have considered yourself a Witch, but now you are affirming your identity and spirituality in front of the Goddess and God. You are asking for their divine inspiration. It is an important step in your magickal life.

When you feel ready, burn the incense and the sage. Anoint
yourself with the salt water, touching your forehead, your heart,
the space just below your navel. Then speak aloud the following:

> *In the name of the Goddess and God,*
> *I come before You on this night*
> *And ask You to witness the rite,*
> *I open my mind and body to the mysteries*
> *Of the universe and of the Self,*
> *I breathe the essence of magick*
> *I taste the fruit of the earth*
> *I see water, sky and what lives within*
> *I hear the song of Cerridwen*
> *By the light of the full moon*
> *I invoke Thee*
> *And call myself Witch*

You may perform any magick after the rite, or you may choose
to spend the remainder of the night in simple meditation.
Follow your instincts. This is a simple but very powerful ritual.
Again, it is your own energy that creates the experience. You
may add to this whatever you wish, but keep the simplicity aspect intact.

Allow the two candles to burn down completely. Scatter any
remnants of wax over the earth early the next day.

Drawing Down the Moon

The act of Drawing Down the Moon from the heavens is a
metaphor for bringing the Goddess into you. It is a ritual often
reserved for covens, but solitary practitioners may perform it as
well. Obviously, it is reserved for the nights of the full moon.

You do not need many accoutrements. The goal of the ritual—to literally become one with the Goddess—is not an easy one to achieve, and it may take several attempts before transcendence seizes you. Again, performing this ritual beneath the moon works best, but if you can't, use a candle while indoors.

Begin by assuming the traditional Goddess pose by forming a *Y* with your body: arms raised and palms opened upward. Ground and center your energy. Close your eyes and imagine the moon's light shooting down from the sky and enveloping you completely. The beams open up your chakra points and stream into your blood.

When you are ready, recite the Charge of the Goddess:

> *Listen to the words of the Great Mother, she who of old has been called Artemis, Astarte, Dione, Melusine, Cerridwen, Diana and by many other names: "Whenever you have need of anything, once in the month, and better it be when the moon is full, then shall ye assemble in some secret place to adore the spirit of Me, who am Queen of all the Wise. You shall be free from slavery, and as a sign that ye be free, you shall sing, dance, feast, make music and love, all in My praise. For Mine is the ecstasy of the spirit, but Mine also is joy on Earth. My law is love unto all beings. Mine is the secret door that opens upon the land of youth, and Mine is the cup of the wine of life that is the Cauldron of Cerridwen, that is the Holy Grail of Immortality. I give the knowledge of the spirit eternal, and beyond death, I give peace, freedom and reunion with those who have gone before. Nor do I demand aught in sacrifice, for behold, I am the Mother of all things, and My love is poured out upon the Earth.*

You may experience any of a number of sensations. It is best to rest a moment and let your body adjust to the enormous power of the invocation. When you feel up to it, perform any magick, as your psychic abilities are in a rare and heightened state.

The Ritual of the American Witch

This ritual is meant to blend the powers of modern-day Witchcraft with those of the American spirit. It is an inspirational rite, a way to further solidify your identity and your spirituality. Perform it on a night when the moon is waxing or full.

Begin by arranging on your altar one red candle, one white candle, and one blue candle. Add to them a small flag or eagle statue. Set two bowls of water on either side of the candles and let these represent our flanking bodies of water.

Ground and center your energy. Think about the meaning of America, our liberty and freedom (especially of religion), and our fallen heroes. We all have much to be thankful for. When you are ready, light the candles and then recite the following:

> *North, South, East and West*
> *Every direction symbolizes the best*
> *Of who I am and where I stand*
> *Firmly rooted in a magical land,*
> *The spirit of nature lives as it should*
> *from shining ocean to mighty Redwood*
> *from rural roads and mountains that dare*
> *to seaside towns and urban flare,*
> *My Native Brother still walks in the forest*
> *My forefathers live in sight and sound*
> *From corners unseen our heroes whisper*
> *And rise above the battled ground,*
> *I walk above it*

Below it
Within it
And through it,
I am a shaper of spirit
And a diviner of mystery
I am an American Witch
Free to be

Chapter Six

Spells, Incantations, and Invocations

A Witch's life is filled with enchanted moments and powerful memories. It is through magick and ritual that we fuse relationships with divinity, our sacred surroundings and ourselves. In the previous chapter, we discussed the meaning of magick—its capabilities and potential, its language as a system based on the very natural forces that govern our world. Here, we will take a closer look at what it means to harness the energy that is alive both within our minds and just beyond them. Casting a spell is not just candlelight and incense. It is about pinpointing a goal, visualizing it and then making it real. It is about intention and will.

Responsibility is of utmost importance when deciding to flex your magickal muscles in accordance with the lunar cycles. You must keep the Wiccan Rede before you at all times, making a conscious choice to tap into your own energy for a positive purpose. To begin, look inside yourself first. What is the goal of your spell? Why are you casting it? After a bit of old-fashioned soul-searching, initiate the design. What tools will you need? Have you chosen a quiet setting where you will not be disturbed? Is the moon in an appropriate phase? Answering these questions will make the road to enchantment a bit smoother.

As with any spell or ritual, you may want to prepare yourself physically and mentally beforehand. Some Witches take ritual baths. Others choose to concentrate on the various accoutrements they will be using later on in the evening. Do whatever it is that will enhance your sense of well-being and confidence. All magickal workings require sound mind and body, and the slightest hint of discord can impede success. A spell is not a minor event. It requires a great deal of energy and exertion. In taking these necessary steps, you are respecting your own abilities and paying homage to the deities you will invoke.

What follows is a sampling of spells for the modern-day practitioner. The breathing exercises included in the previous chapter should be performed to relax and balance the mind. Of course, you may have already developed your own methods of grounding and concentration, and if these bring comfort, stick to them. When reviewing any of these spells, keep in mind that adding certain herbal ingredients or changing a moon phase may alter the results. Spells that draw money, attract luck or healing energy should be performed when the moon is waxing or full. Spells that banish negativity, ill fortune, disease or unwanted habits should be performed when the moon is waning.

Visualize your goals. See the reality. And, most significantly, believe in the magick.

Spells for Luck and Good Fortune

The New Moon Spell for Luck

You will need: A white candle
Scented oil, of your choosing
2 basil leaves
A rose petal
A sprinkling of salt

On a night of the new moon, construct an altar beneath or beside a window. Take the white candle—to honor the Goddess—and anoint it with the scented oil. Place it in its holder in the very center of the altar. On either side of it, lay down the basil leaves and the rose petal.

Begin by meditating for a few minutes. Breathe deeply. Ground and center your energy. When you feel calm and fully at ease, cast your circle. Sprinkle the salt directly over the altar. Then light the candle and repeat the following incantation:

> *Goddess of power, Goddess of might*
> *Hear my words borne on the moonlight,*
> *I invoke thee now with strength and skill*
> *Bless my mind with Your divine will*
> *By sacred fire and nascent moon*
> *Luck will come to grant this boon*

Spend as much time as possible concentrating on the intent of your spell. Pinpoint the areas of your life that need a smattering of good luck and then visualize the positive changes. Remember that the candle and accompanying incantation are tools. It is your mind that possesses the true power to manifest good fortune.

Open your eyes and sit for a minute or two before the glowing flame. Take the basil leaves in your hands and meditate upon their color. Green is most often associated with luck and money. Let your energy flow into the leaves. When you're done, replace them on the altar.

Repeat the step with the rose petal. This time, let the red or pink color guide you to notions of self-worth and love.

Once the candle has burned down completely, gather what little wax remains and bury it in the ground with the basil and rose petal. This is symbolic of returning your knowledge and cementing your will to the earth. Luck will come to you.

A Basic Crystal Spell

You will need: A quartz crystal
A white handkerchief
A green thread, at least 12 inches long

When the moon is waxing—and all the better if it is in the astrological sign of Taurus—retire to a quiet corner and gather the above-mentioned items. Spread the handkerchief out before you. The green thread should be placed horizontally on top of the handkerchief. Set the crystal down just below the thread.

Begin with a breathing and meditation exercise. Invoke the Goddess and God. Summon the elements. When you are in a relaxed frame of mind, take the crystal in your hands and recite the following incantation:

North, East, South and West,
Aid me in this clear request
Thread to knot, these words I say
And so good fortune will come my way

Spend several minutes concentrating on your desire as you hold the crystal. Envision the white light of the moon pulsing around it. See the four elements encircling you. They are present as gnomes, sylphs, salamanders and undines. Continue to summon them in your mind as your meditation grows deeper.

Next, set the crystal down on the handkerchief. Set the thread aside. Begin folding the handkerchief neatly over the crystal, until both are joined in a tight little square. Then go to work with the thread, tying it around the handkerchief-wrapped crystal. Make several knots as you continue to envision your luck changing. The thread should seal off any open edges on the handkerchief.

The charm you have made is now infused with magickal

properties and your own invoked desires. Wear it on your person or place it in your briefcase or purse. You may also set it inside your home; in this case, be certain to put it where you will see it every morning—on a desktop or nightstand, perhaps on a bureau. Meditate on it daily.

A Candle Spell for Good Fortune

You will need: A green candle
Incense, of your choosing
A glass of spring or bottled water
An almond
An athame or needle

The candle-and-needle spell is quite common. In traditional British Wicca, the needle is sometimes inserted directly into the wax, but here you will need it only for inscription purposes.

On a night when the moon is waxing, construct an altar using the above-mentioned items. The candle and its holder should go in the center. In the lower right corner, place the stick of incense alongside its burner. To left of the candle, set down the glass of water and the single almond. Align the needle or athame so that it is just in front of the candle.

Begin with a breathing exercise. Close your eyes and ground yourself. This spell requires a bit more verve, so spending adequate time in silent meditation is a good idea.

When you are ready, cast your circle accordingly. Light the incense. Hold the needle or athame and start visualizing the goal of your spell. Then take the candle and slowly and carefully etch your name and birth date into the wax. Sketch out a pentacle as well. Pass the candle through the smoke of the incense before depositing it back into its holder. Light it.

Begin meditating again, but this time keep your eyes open and concentrate on the glowing fire. As your focus intensifies, you may notice the flame shooting upright. This indicates a direct current linking your energy to that of the candle. Invoke the Goddess and God in any way that suits you. Perhaps you might want to recite the Charge of the Goddess. Sometimes simply speaking to deity works as well. Ask for luck and good fortune. Communicate sincerely and honestly.

Next, take the almond and drop it into the glass of water. (Almonds, sacred to Mercury, are believed to hold luck-drawing properties.) Hold the glass before you so that it is backlit by the candle's flame. This should help you visualize the moon clearly. Draw the lunar energy into the glass, seeing its rays plunge through the clear fluid. Drink the water and eat the almond.

Go back to your meditation again, spending as much time as possible envisioning the powers of luck and how they will help improve your life. Let the candle burn itself out. Any remaining wax should be consigned to the earth.

The Spell of Jupiter

You will need: An orange candle
                  A yellow pouch
                  Cinquefoil
                  Aniseeds
                  Ginger

Jupiter is the planet most often associated with luck. Its influences are known to attract benevolent forces, money and prosperity. On a night of the waxing moon, and better still if it is in the astrological sign of Jupiter, perform the following simple spell.

In a quiet setting, light the orange candle and spend a few minutes in meditation. Reflect on the energy of Jupiter. Imagine it aligned perfectly with the growing moon, the conjoined power emanating from the sky to encircle you. Take the yellow pouch and hold it open with one hand. With the other, gather the cinquefoil and hold it in your open palm; pass it over the candle flame three times, then drop it into the pouch. Repeat the process with the aniseeds and ginger.

When you are done, drop a bit of wax into the pouch before sealing it. Hang the pouch in your home, either above a doorway or window. It can also be placed beneath a bed or beside a mirror. Allow the orange candle to burn out completely and bury the remaining wax.

A Money Spell

You will need: A one-dollar bill
A black or blue pen
A teaspoon of ground cinnamon
A tonka bean

On a night of the waxing moon, spread a crisp one-dollar bill over a flat surface and, using the pen, inscribe your initials and birth date into each of the four corners. On the back of the bill, write the following verse:

On a Witch's night my luck does fly
By moon and magick this bill will multiply

Sprinkle the cinnamon over the front of the dollar bill. Drop the tonka bean into the center. Then roll the bill into a scroll, folding the open ends together. The charm works best if it is buried beside an oak or evergreen tree close to your home. If you live in an apartment or at a far distance from any natural setting, wrap the charm in a small piece of flannel and place it on your windowsill.

The Clover Spell

> You will need: A mason jar
> A four-leaf clover
> Apple seeds
> Honeysuckle petals

This simple spell will require you to fill the mason jar with water from a running river, brook or stream. Do this twenty-four hours before a night when the moon is in a waxing phase. Fill the jar to within an inch or two of its mouth and seal it. Keep the jar in a cool place.

On the appointed evening, find a quiet place and begin the spell with a breathing exercise. Charge the clover by holding it and meditating for several minutes. Concentrate on each of the leaves. Let the four points represent the elements of earth, air fire and water.

Drop the apple seeds and the honeysuckle petals into the mason jar, and then add the clover. Reseal the jar. Add this mixture to your bath, or use it to anoint candles, amulets and charms. The honeysuckle flower is sacred to Jupiter, and apple seeds have long been associated with the Goddess. The clover, of course, has a colorful history for attracting luck. Blending these basic ingredients together will harness the forces of good fortune to your side.

The Aventurine Charm Spell

You will need: A white votive candle
                Musk oil
                A green votive candle
                An aventurine stone
                A twelve-inch black cord

Aventurine is immensely powerful where luck spells are concerned. To make a charm that will maximize its potency, perform
the following spell on a night when the moon is waxing.

Anoint the white votive candle with musk oil and light it to
honor the Goddess. Anoint the green candle and light it to honor
the element of earth. Handle the aventurine with great care, and
begin the spell by meditating upon the stone's properties.

Think of luck, but go a bit deeper by drawing comparisons
between the earth's ability to produce the aventurine and your
own desire for positive vibes. Like the geological process, luck
sometimes forms in bits and pieces, chunks and splinters. In
order for it to come together, it has to be melded, sculpted, chis-
eled just so. Let the metaphor guide you. Visualize your luck as
emanating from the ground, spinning and coiling and breaking
through the soil. Imagine yourself finding it as you would a precious stone and picking it up.

Feel your way around the smoothness of the aventurine, not-
ing the slightest curves and ridges along its edge. Keep that concrete image of luck in your mind. Understand it as a natural
process born from the natural forces of the universe. It is alive in
your hands, ten pinpricks of sparkling light. It is real and pure
and physical. Very slowly, link that image of luck with the aventurine in your hands. See the two merging. Feel your own pulse
beating against the stone. Draw it close to the candles and let
their combined heat circle the aventurine.

Recite the following incantation:

Sacred stone and earthen best
Let my vision manifest,
Luck is mine at every hour
And so I claim its natural power

Take the black cord and wrap it around the aventurine. Knot it once, and make certain the ends of the cord are not long and flowing. When the candle has burned down bury the remaining wax.

Carry the charm on your person and repeat the incantation every morning.

A Parchment Spell

You will need: A sheet of parchment paper
A blue candle
A green-ink pen

Words, when written or spoken, are effective tools. This spell is highly personal and can be cast for luck or to manifest any other change in your life.

When the moon is waxing, write out your innermost dreams and desires on a sheet of parchment paper. Do this by the light of a blue candle. Use green ink because it is representative of prosperity, good fortune and abundance. You may construct a letter to the Gods or a specific deity. It may also be a simple list describing your needs, be they material, emotional or physical. Don't hold anything back. Write as if all your hopes depended on this very sheet of paper. Are you seeking a new career or a boost in finances? Do you need some luck in your home and family life? Purge your mind of all that is hidden from the outside world.

When you are done, personalize the paper all the more by inscribing on it your name and birth date three times. Then fold it three times. Hold the paper close to the candle's flame and invoke the Triple Moon Goddess. As Maiden, she is like the dreams and desire you have held within you—energetic, new, blazing with possibility. She is the Mother at this very moment, maturing and strengthening, just like the words and emotions you have written. In her Crone aspect, she represents the wisdom that comes from fruition and knowledge, from the realization of dreams and the lessons they have imparted. Meditate on each of these aspects. By bringing what lives inside your private self out into the physical realm, you are recognizing your own self-worth and capability. You are also consciously mapping out a plan of action.

Spend as much time as you need performing this spell. Do not be hindered by notions of exposure or embarrassment—no one will ever see your writings. When you are done and fully satisfied with your words, burn the parchment and let the ashes take to the wind. Thus, your words are being carried off into the atmosphere and solidified by the forces of nature. When the candle has burned down, bury the remaining wax.

A Roman Deity Spell

You will need: A green candle
                 A yellow or gold candle
                 A teaspoon of nutmeg
                 A sprig of rue
                 A handful of soil from your garden or yard
                 A small bowl

Fortuna was a Roman Goddess of prosperity, bounty and abundance. It was once believed that paying her homage would ensure a full harvest. Throughout the ages, she has been a symbol of good fortune and luck, social status, material riches and wealth.

On a night of the full or waxing moon, arrange your altar with the two candles, nutmeg and rue. The handful of soil should already be in the small bowl. Begin with a breathing and meditation exercise. Ground and center your energy.

Next, the candles. Light the yellow or gold one and say: *I honor Fortuna, Goddess of luck and prosperity, as golden and bright as the sun that warms me.*

Light the green candle and say: *As this flame burns, so too does my positive luck. I honor Fortuna, rushing over the bountiful earth, as bright as the moonlight that guides me.*

Hold the bowl up to the candles and sprinkle a pinch of soil onto the altar. Then mix the nutmeg into the soil slowly, visualizing the process of germination and growth. The nutmeg represents your own essence; as it blends with the earth, picture it fusing into every tiny grain of soil.

Take the sprig of rue and hold it up so that it is eye level with the candles. Recite the following incantation:

> *When earth and spirit join as one*
> *The soul's bounty is firmly done,*
> *I invoke Fortuna*
> *To brighten my way*
> *And let good fortune always stay!*

Gently mix the sprig of rue into the soil and nutmeg. Leave the bowl on your altar until the candles burn down completely. Early the next morning, bury the remaining wax, and sift the mixture back into the earth, either into your own garden or in a corner of the yard where it will not be disturbed.

A Full Moon Prosperity Spell

> You will need: A white candle
> A small glass bottle
> Lavender
> 2 Bay leaves
> Pine needles
> Moon Goddess oil

At the full moon, the Goddess is at her most powerful, and so too are the Witches who pay her homage. It is a time for ritual and magick. Any desire can be attained on this eve, but prosperity is perhaps the most popular. We all want to better ourselves and our lives. This easy spell can help you do just that.

All full moon magick should begin with the invocation of the Goddess and God. Try to relax your mind and body as much as possible. Speak aloud your wish for prosperity and how you envision it changing your life. It may be for finances or love, career or self-confidence. Be direct and true. Do not hold anything back.

Gather the above-mentioned items on your altar and then light the candle. Start by charging the small glass bottle. See in it your own reflection. Trace a pentagram over each side with your fingertip. Pass the bottle over the candle flame quickly three times.

One by one, drop the lavender, bay leaves and pine needles into the bottle. You do not need much—just enough to coat the bottom. Give it a shake. If you are close to a window or—better yet—outside, hold the bottle up to the full moon and let the essence of the Goddess envelop you. Sit before your altar and spend several minutes meditating on your intended goal while cradling the bottle in your hands.

Add the oil so that the lavender, bay leaves and pine needles are submerged. Don't fill the bottle to the rim—less than halfway is fine. Cap the bottle and set it on your altar. Let it sit as the candle burns down completely; later, bury the remaining wax.

Place the bottle in your window to draw prosperity to you. Later, the oil can be used in small amounts to anoint candles when casting other spells and performing rituals. With each time you use the oil, prosperous energies are growing stronger.

Spells for Love

The Flower Spell

> You will need: Rose petals
> Dandelion petals
> A strand of your own hair
> A white letter-size envelope
> A twelve-inch red ribbon

We all hope for love. Some find it early in life and others are still searching after twenty years of single-hood. The majority of people stand firm in their beliefs that the Right One is out there, waiting to be claimed. That's probably true, but sometimes we need a little help from the Gods to get the wheels of love turning. This simple spell will get the job done nicely.

On a night of the waxing or full moon, place the rose and dandelion petals and the strand of hair into a white envelope that has never been used. Seal the flap. Then hold the envelope in your hands and recite the following incantation:

> *By heart and moon and pure desire,*
> *Earth, Air, Water and Fire*
> *Love abounds, day and night*
> *My Innermost now takes flight,*

I cast this spell, a circle round
What I seek will soon be found

Tie the ribbon around the envelope and knot it twice. Spend time meditating on the meaning of love and how it will create positive changes in your life. In the midnight hour, place the envelope beneath your bed, or tape it behind a mirror. Let it stay undisturbed.

A Basic Candle Spell for Love

You will need: A red candle
                 A needle or athame
                 A few celery seeds
                 3 pebbles

On a night when the moon is waxing or full, take the red candle and, using a thin needle or your athame, inscribe your name and birth date into the wax. Sketch a heart, pentagram or any other symbol that holds personal meaning to you. Hold the candle in your hands and say:

I charge this candle as a magickal tool for love.
My desire is pure. My energy is strong.
What I seek, I will find.

Light the candle. While meditating, hold the celery seeds and the pebbles in the palm of your right hand; cup your left hand over them and chant the following incantation:

Stone and seed
And earth in a row,
Let the magick sow and grow

After the candle has burned out completely, gather any loose particles of wax. At dawn, bury the pebbles and the celery seeds in a straight line, vertically. Beside them, consign the remaining wax.

The Oak Tree Love Spell

You will need: A teaspoon of rosemary
A teaspoon of salt
A small glass jar
A cup of red wine
3 cherries

Before beginning this spell, you will need to find a big old oak tree. If you have one on your own property, all the better. If not, the tree should be in a secluded, wooded setting, because you don't want your magick to be disturbed. This spell is performed in two stages: the first half at night, the second half early the next day.

On the eve before the full moon, mix together the rosemary and salt in the glass jar. Cast a circle, putting the jar in the center. Sit before it and invoke the Goddess and God, envisioning the goal of your love spell. Once again, don't hold anything back. Let the floodgates open.

Add the wine to the jar. Slowly eat the cherries, and then drop the pits into the jar. Seal it. Give it a few good shakes and, if possible, go out and hold it under the moonlight. Bring the jar back inside with you and set it to rest on your bureau or nightstand while you sleep.

Early the next day, take the jar back to the oak tree. Ground and center your energy. Walk clockwise around the tree three times, once again harnessing the forces of the Goddess and God. Remember that in the outdoors, you are in presence of the

Horned God and the elements. Let nature speak to you. Feeling
that divine connecting to earth and sky is as much a spell as any
you will perform within a magick circle. Concentrate on the link
between nature and the very natural intent of your goal. Love is
what brings forth abundance and life. Like the tiniest bud or
tallest evergreen, it begins with a seed.

Stand motionless in front of the oak tree and speak aloud your
desire. Then gently tap the jar against the bark a few times.
Kneel in the dirt and slowly dig a hole as close to the tree as possible. Bury the jar. Thank the Goddess and God and then walk
away without looking back.

To Keep a Relationship Strong

> You will need: A male-shaped candle
> A female-shaped candle
> A cup of sugar
> A small red box

If you are in a relationship and wish to keep it going smoothly
and sweetly, perform this spell on a night when the moon is waxing and in the astrological sign of Taurus. Male- and female-
shaped candles can be purchased at any occult supply shop.
They should be white or red. For same-sex relationships, simply
use same-sex candles. Gender is symbolic here; the love shared
by two individuals is what truly energizes this spell.

Set the two candles on your altar. Spread the sugar around
them in a circle. As you light each one, speak your name and the
name of your beloved. Sit before the altar and meditate upon the
relationship, concentrating on all that is wonderful and sublime.
Channel your energy into keeping a healthy flow between the
two of you. Ask the Goddess and God to continue solidifying
those desires, or simply communicate with deity through recent

memories you and your beloved have shared. Let the candles burn down completely. Then gather up the sugar and remaining wax and scatter it all into the small red box. Set the box beneath or beside your bed.

To dress the spell up a bit, you may add photographs or other small tokens to the altar—anything that is representative of the relationship.

A Holly Spell for Love

You will need: A small branch or sprig of holly
                 A pink cloth, about the size of a
                    handkerchief
                 A needle
                 Red thread

To draw love into your life, perform this spell on a night when the moon is waxing or full. It is simple but powerful. It is also time-consuming and methodical. Make certain to clear your mind beforehand, as any distractions can hinder your results.

Take the branch or sprig of holly and press it to the pink cloth. Close your eyes. Visualize the goal of your spell. Charge the holly with your essence and speak aloud your desire.

Next, pick up the needle and thread. As you slip the thread into the eye of the needle, say:

> *My senses sharp, my heart aware*
> *I choose to care and love and dare*

Begin stitching the holly into the cloth. Go around the leaves, letting the thread wrap around the entire sprig or small branch. It doesn't have to look neat. Sew as much as you need and, while doing so, keep your mind focused on the topic of love. Continue visualizing. When you're done, put the cloth beside your bed-room window for one night, and then carry the charm in your purse, briefcase or pocket.

A Spell for Lovers

You will need: A purple candle
A drop of lavender oil
Jasmine seeds
Gardening soil
A small planting pot

This spell is especially powerful for newlyweds or any couple moving into a new home or apartment.

On a night of the full moon, arrange the above items on your altar, with the candle in the upper left corner. Again, you may heighten the magick by adding photographs or personal tokens, which should be placed around the candle. Ground and center your energy. Get in to a relaxed state of mind. Call upon the four elements to aid you in the spell.

Anoint the candle with the lavender oil and light it. Then go about planting the seeds in the normal fashion, adding the soil into the pot accordingly. As you do this, say the following:

> *From earth to sky to flowing ocean*
> *Let love keep its fluid motion*
> *From seed to soil to blooming flower*
> *I hold within this sacred power*

Place the pot in your window or, if possible, directly beneath the moon's light. Let the candle burn out completely.

Keep a close eye on the budding plant. Meditate with it each day and repeat the above incantation each night before turning in to bed. When the flowers have bloomed, transfer the pot to your garden. This ends the cycle of the spell, and it should be repeated every time you add a new, glowing plant to your garden.

The Venus Love Spell

You will need: 2 pink candles
A white votive candle
Violets
A bowl of water
Bergamot oil

This spell should be performed on a night when the moon is waxing and in the astrological sign of Pisces. It also honors Venus, Goddess of love.

Begin by setting up your altar. The three pink candles sit in the center, forming a half circle. In front of them place the white votive candle. The violets should rest beside the bowl of water. You will only need two or three drops of the bergamot oil.

After grounding and centering your energy, light the white candle and recite the following incantation to Venus:

> *Great Goddess of love and splendor*
> *and the heart's surrender,*
> *Supreme Venus of the heavens,*
> *Within you flows the fount of passion*
> *and the rivers of affection,*
> *Awaken in me Your golden fire*
> *So that I might know true desire*
> *made real and strong and everlasting,*
> *Goddess of the Innermost*
> *Guardian of all Beloved,*
> *Hear me now and always*

Anoint the two pink candles with the bergamot oil. Light them.
Then drop the violets into the water and let the bowl sit on the
altar, untouched, until the candles burn down. Scatter any remnants of wax into the wind.

The next day, bottle the water and add it to your bath. Dab a
drop on your bed and smear a bit of it across any mirror in your
home.

An Amulet Spell for Attracting the Opposite Sex

> You will need: A blue candle
>   A bloodstone
>   A cup of ginseng tea

This spell should be performed on a night of the waxing moon.
Take a ritual bath before settling in to your sacred space, as it
will help put you in a more confident state of mind. You will be
meditating on love, but also on physical attraction. It is generally
not a good idea to cast a spell on a specific person because this
can interfere with one's karma, so if you have a specific person in
sight, try to keep your magick as general as possible. The old
adage applies here: if it's meant to be, it will happen. In the
meantime, this fast and easy spell can only heighten the energy
around you.

Light the blue candle and spend several minutes concentrating on your own well-being. Blue is the color most often associated with thought and self-expression. This stage of the spell is
about you. What is it you are projecting for? Do you want a hot
fling, a no-strings mate who will rock your physical needs? Or is
it a long-term, relationship-oriented person you are seeking? It's
important to put your desire into focus—the more direct you are
in magick, the better your results.

Stay connected to the blue candle a bit longer. Study yourself thoroughly, considering how you feel physically and mentally. Are you in a healthy place, fully capable of giving to someone else as much as you hope to receive? Do you feel confident about your appearance? Weigh any and everything that may be standing in the way of attracting the opposite sex. Deep down, we all have our insecurities. Now is the time to deal with them. Once they are realized, you will have a better perspective of what you want for yourself and in another person.

Next, hold the bloodstone in your hands, raising it up so that it is backlit by the candle's flame. Imagine it as being suspended in the night sky, a perfect moon illuminating its shape. Close your fingers over the stone and recite the following:

> *I draw the magnetic powers of the earth*
> *into my body*
> *I am one with myself*
> *and with another*

Drink the tea. Leave the stone beside the candle, and let the candle burn down completely. Later, bury the remaining wax. Carry the stone with you wherever you go; it is an amulet, charged with your own essence and energy. For added verve, recite the above incantation every morning before leaving your home.

The Sex Spell

You will need: 2 red votive candles
Cinnamon oil
An athame
A cup of red wine
A handful of rice

This spell is intended to enrich one's sex life. It works regardless of gender, so those in same-sex relationships will reap the mag-ickal benefits just as well as any man and woman. For added potency, you may want to perform this spell in the nude (a.k.a. *skyclad*).

On a night of the full moon, gather the above items on your altar. Begin by grounding and centering your energy. When you are in a relaxed state of mind, anoint the two votive candles with the cinnamon oil. Apply a drop of the oil to the base of your spine and another drop just beneath your navel. Light the candles. Meditate on your desire for a more heightened sex life. Picture your beloved and think about the last time you made love.

Next, pick up your athame. Grasp the handle tightly and turn it so that it is pointing downward, directly over the cup of wine. Slowly but firmly, plunge the athame into the wine. Holding it in place, recite the following incantation:

> *Body to mind*
> *and soul to flesh,*
> *With this spell I feel the caress*
> *of heat and hands and lips as one*
> *By sacred magick, let it be done!*

Remove the athame from the cup. Take a few sips of the wine. Gather the rice in your hands and charge the grains. Envision them brimming with the red radiance of sensuality and ecstasy.

Draw a bath and carry one of the votive candles into the bathroom. Throw the handful of rice into the warm water. Immerse yourself in a relaxing few minutes, still concentrating on your intended goal.

Later, transfer both candles and whatever wine remains with you to the bedroom. Let your beloved take a sip. If possible, get into the mood and set some motion to the ocean.

Spells for Protection and Banishing

A Waning Moon Spell

You will need: A black candle
A white candle
A clove of garlic
Caraway seeds
A brown or black flannel pouch

Every now and then, we all fall victim to negative vibes. They might hit you at work or in your career path. Perhaps you and your beloved have been walking on some rocky ground. Most often, negativity affects us physically and emotionally through headaches, exhaustion and unexplained fatigue. When the moon is waning, spells should be cast to neutralize any negativity and banish a stream of nasty luck.

So, on a night of the waning moon, gather the above items on your altar and begin by grounding and centering your energy. If you feel out of sorts, this may be difficult. It is imperative that you transcend any sense of malaise because you don't want to impart that weakened energy into the spell. Take as much time as you need aligning your mind and body. Forget what ails you and remember that when sitting before your altar surrounded by the accoutrements of magick, you are in sacred space. The Goddess and God are already listening.

Tune your mental energy to the four elements. Summon them and ask them to guard your rites. Calmly light the black candle and recite the following:

> *In the name of the Goddess and God*
> *and every protective deity,*
> *I banish all negativity,*

Gone are my ills
of mind
heart
soul

Envision an amorphous shadow beside you. Picture a stream of white light shooting from your hands and circling around the shadow, eventually overpowering it. Take the thing down.

Spend a few minutes meditating and collecting your energy once again. When you are ready, light the white candle and recite the following:

Light
and power
and positive force,
Spiral upward from the source
Neutralize all harm, misfortune and bane unseen,
In the name of the Goddess and God who reign Supreme

Gather the clove of garlic and the caraway seeds and place them in the flannel pouch. Pass the pouch over the candle flames three times, and then set it on the altar as both candles burn down; later, bury the remaining wax.

At sunrise the next day, throw the pouch into a river, stream or moving body of water.

The Sacred Pentacle Spell

You will need: A large pentacle, either drawn on paper
or a stone disk
A light blue candle
A cup of salt water

On a night of the waning moon, sit in a quiet room and place the pentagram on the floor before you. Study it for a while, concentrating on its true meaning and its historical relevance. As we have seen, the pentagram symbolizes the human body. It is also the four elements and the four directions surmounted by the Spirit—the combined energies of the Goddess and God. Its origins are believed to date back to Paleolithic times. Today, the pentagram symbolizes modern-day Witchcraft. In addition to mysticism and divinity, it is used for protection.

When you are ready, begin the spell by lighting the light blue candle. Dip your finger into the cup of salt water and, starting clockwise, press it to the first point on the pentagram. Hold it there and say:

> *The Goddess and God are within me,*
> *I am always safe,*
> *I walk on solid ground*
> *One with nature and divinity*

Dip your finger into the cup again and press it to the next point. Hold it there firmly and say:

> *The power of the West hears me,*
> *I am one with the element of water*
> *Sacred undines, I summon thee*

Dip your finger into the cup a third time and press it to the next point, saying:

> *The power of the South hears me,*
> *I am one with the element of fire*
> *Sacred salamanders, I summon thee*

Dip your finger into the cup a fourth time and press it to the next point of the pentagram, saying:

> *The power of the North hears me,*
> *I am one with the element of earth*
> *Sacred gnomes, I summon thee*

Dip your finger into the cup a fifth time and press it to the last point, saying:

> *The power of the East hears me,*
> *I am one with the element of air*
> *Sacred Sylphs, I summon thee*

Finally, dip your finger into the cup again, and this time anoint yourself with the sign of the pentagram: forehead, right nipple, left shoulder, right shoulder, left nipple and forehead once again.

Meditate. Breathe slowly and evenly. Relax. Envision a circle of white and blue light surrounding you. Then see the circle doubling and tripling, until it is a spiral wrapping your entire body. Stand up before the altar. The light is a vortex of protection, shielding you from all harm and negativity. Staring down at the pentagram, recite the following incantation:

> *The Goddess guards me,*
> *The God guides me,*
> *One with nature, I know and see*

Thank the elements and release them. Let the candle burn out completely before burying the remaining wax.

A Binding Spell

You will need: A black candle
A piece of black cloth or tarp
A puppet or straw doll
Black cord
Crushed basil
½ teaspoon of black pepper

The Witch's Rede—*harm none, do what you will*—prevents practitioners from using magick geared toward danger or violence. The binding spell, however, is a mechanism for self-defense. The act of binding through magick does not imply ill will. It is, rather, a way of keeping a person's negativity at bay.

Perform this spell on a night when the moon is waning. Arrange the items on your altar, and then spend a significant amount of time grounding and centering your energy. Begin by neutralizing any harmful forces. Picture a vortex of protective white light spinning around you. Say out loud:

I neutralize all negativity. I am safe within this circle.
The Goddess and God protect me.

Light the black candle. Spread the black cloth or tarp over the altar. Hold the puppet or straw doll in your hands and name it. Who is the person you are binding? Why are you binding that person? Visualize the negative traits and characteristics that you wish to block. Then take the black cord and very slowly start winding it around the puppet's feet and legs. As you do this, say:

I bind your feet and legs, (the person's name)
You cannot approach me or do me harm

Keep the cord moving steadily upward, around the puppet's
hands and arms. Say:

> *I bind your hands and arms,* (the person's name)
> *You cannot touch or feel me*

Wrap the cord around the puppet's head, saying:

> *I bind your thoughts,* (the person's name)
> *You cannot think of me negatively*

Hold the puppet in your hands again, envisioning a gray stream
of light firmly wrapping around it. Firmly slam it down on the
altar, over the cloth or tarp.

Next, sprinkle the crushed basil and black pepper over the puppet. Fold the tarp over it, so that all four corners meet in the center.
Tie a knot around it once. Pick it up and pass it through the candle's
flame. Set it down again and recite the following incantation:

> *Magick bind, negativity end*
> *Herb and candle start to mend*
> *Ill will gone and danger vanish*
> *Darkness and shadow I hereby banish!*

Leave the cloth-wrapped puppet on your altar until the candle
burns down completely. Early the next day, bury it and the remaining wax where they will not be disturbed.

Spells for Healing

A Basic Healing Spell

You will need: A white candle
A quartz crystal
Mint leaves

This simple spell is intended to heal minor physical or emotional ailments. It is important to remember that no matter a Witch's power and magick, conventional medicine should never be ignored or dismissed. Healing plays a significant role in the life of every Witch, but we are all still human and must therefore abide by the advancements of modern medicine. When casting a spell or performing a ritual, keep in mind that you are aiding in your own, or another person's, recovery. Here, again, the spiritual and the scientific must merge.

On a night of the full moon, sit in a quiet place and begin with a meditation exercise. Concentrate on where you are directing your healing energy. Is it for you or for another person? Is it physical or emotional? Pinpoint the area of the mind or body first, and then light the white candle.

Raise your energy. Ground and center it. Visualization is the key to healing, and you are harnessing the white, shimmering light of the universe coming into your own body and pulsing from your hands. When you feel the heat prickling over your palms, pick up the quartz crystal and enclose it in your hands, saying:

I charge this crystal with divine healing energy
In the name of the Goddess and God and
the combined powers of
Earth, Air, Fire and Water
As I will it, I am healed.

Place the crystal before the candle. Leave the room and brew a tea from the mint leaves, letting it steep for at least five minutes. Mint is a healing herb. Its aroma and taste are a rejuvenating source for the immune system. Drink the tea before the candle and crystal, and then carry the crystal with you as an amulet. If you are casting this spell for another person, simply brew the tea for and transfer over the amulet to that person. Later, bury the remaining wax.

To Heal a Broken Heart

> You will need: A white votive candle
> A blue votive candle
> Leaves from an oak tree
> A small heart-shaped box
> A tablespoon of honey

Perform this spell on a night of the new moon. It is a personal rite, meant to help mend the pangs that so often accompany the aftermath of a bad relationship and its subsequent breakup.

Begin by concentrating on the relationship itself. This probably will be a painful process, but in order to heal, you must first recognize the source of your pain and confront it. Ask yourself the most difficult questions. Why did it come to an end? What part, if any, did you play in the ending of the relationship? Meditate on these points, honestly and sincerely.

Then concentrate on the future. What positive effects will the severing of these ties have? There were most likely unhealthy aspects of the relationship, and as they pass out of your life, meditate on what this means for you. How has the relationship changed you? How will you grow? What lessons have you learned?

Light the candles. Invoke the Goddess, thinking of her in her

Crone aspect. She is old but full of wisdom. She has lived and learned. And yet, at the core of her being is a golden light, a wellspring of strength and courage. You may feel broken and detached from the world, but this sense of despondency will soon end. Our emotions, like nature, are also moving in a constant cycle.

Drop the leaves into the small heart-shaped box. Drizzle the honey over them, saying:

> *I look for strength in the never-ending Wheel,*
> *I find in myself the power to heal*
> *Maiden, Mother and all-knowing Crone*
> *In your presence I am never alone*

Leave the box in the shadows of the candles until they burn down completely. The next day, throw the box and remaining wax into a river or moving body of water.

Healing for Another

You will need: A white candle
Sage
A bunch of parsley
Mint
A pinch of cinnamon
A photograph of the person to whom
you are sending healing energy

On a night of the full moon, gather the above items and set up your altar. Begin by lighting the white candle. Burn the sage as an incense for purification, letting the faint wisps of smoke swirl around the bunch of parsley, and the mint and cinnamon, saying:

By the divine light of the Goddess and God
I cleanse the circle that surrounds me
and charge it with
the healing energies of the earth

Pick up the photograph of the person you are directing your
healing energy toward. Close your eyes and envision a stream of
white light pouring from your third eye (just between your eye-
brows) and onto the photograph. Spend several minutes concentrating.

Set the photograph down on the altar, very close to the burning candle. Take the bunch of parsley and begin to slowly
"sweep" the photograph in a clockwise motion. Then sweep several times in the shape of a pentagram. As you do this, chant the
following incantation:

I cast this spell
to make you well
and cleanse away the pain,
The Goddess heals you
The God energizes you
Your body is anew

Sprinkle the cinnamon over the photograph. If you have mint
leaves, place them on top of the photograph; if the mint is
crushed (as if from a tea bag), sprinkle this as well.

Leave everything on the altar until the candle has burned
down. Keep the photograph of the person close to a window.

The Invocations

To Invoke the Goddess

Great Goddess of the Universe
of sea and sky and spirit
of earth and air, fire and water
of night and day and moon and sun,
of all that is and will be done,
You who are huntress and mother,
death and rebirth,
Hear my words in this hour
and grant me
every hidden power:
The knowledge that lives within me
the courage to dare fearlessly
the sight to see what cannot be seen
and hear the patter of every trickling stream,
the voice of the wind will whisper
and lead me to my Innermost desire,
where Your mystery brims with magick
and the promise of achieving higher,
Goddess of the Dawn,
of dew and mist and birdsong,
granter of light and warmth,
of breeze and rain and mist,
Be with me in this moment
as You are at the start
of each new day:
cresting above the horizon and the trees
the mountains and the valleys
the wooded paths and
concrete crossroads,

Great Goddess of the Dark,
of shadow and substance
and the new tomorrow,
of starlight and black skies
of midnight beauty and gracious moon
of the universal womb,
I invoke Thee as I stand
Between time and place,
An instrument of Your
Enchanted grace

To Invoke the God

In the woods and forests
Your Spirit walks,
and so the kingdom
breathes and talks
Running wild in silent flow
As above, so below,
Great God of Nature
of grass and soil,
of seeds and thorns,
of branch and leaf and guiding horns,
I invoke Thee now as
the circle is cast,
moment to moment, present and past:
Osiris, Janus, Cernunnos
and Pan,
God of the green
Of beast and man,
the sun-washed fields
unleash your bounty,
the light of day

colors your path,
the winds will stir and the leaves
will fall,
the seasons turn as you
complete the All,
Yours is the Law of
harmony and strength,
Of beginnings and endings,
Great Father of the Earth
And the sacred hunt,
From deep within
Your power of motion,
I offer You my every emotion,
fear and passion and
sorrow and mirth,
Yours is the essence of
Blessed Rebirth

A Witch's Invocation for Self-Empowerment

Down through a sky colored by night,
The moon's long fingers flex their might,
Into the forests it churns and turns
Pure as the silver of a thousand lakes—
Give praise to the earth as
The Goddess wakes

Isis, Inanna, Artemis and Brid,
Harken now to the sacred Creed,
She darkens in shadow
She disperses like fire
She emerges from the depths of
Truest desire

Breathing Her essence is tasting the core
Of birth and death and ancient lore
Summon the wind,
Sample the flower
Gaze upon the stars
And treasure Her power

In olden days She reigned supreme
Whispered in honor but never seen,
The Temples of Egypt hammered in gold
The Roman ruins nestled deep in the fold
Of a story, a history
A mystery
As yet to be told

They walked in fields overflowing with grain,
They parted their lips to guzzle the rain
Warmth from the dance of a single flame
And silken air to wash away the pain
Of sudden scorn and
Unspeakable fear
Silenced in blood by an Inquisitor's spear

But still She stayed
Clandestine and meek,
Told amid centuries never to speak
Yet rising slowly to a fiery peak—
Listen well,
Oh—can you hear it?
"Return to Me, For I am the Spirit"

Waxing, Waning
New and Full,
When black descends

Feel the pull
Of moonlit ties and a limitless embrace
And worship the ground of whatever place

Deep in the mind, within the heart,
The circle spins without end or start,
Ride the crescendo, hear the pitch
Know the tale of the Eternal Witch

Her children gather on this eve
Eager to spark the magic they weave,
By sired herb or Witch's spell
They plumb the cloak of the earth's dark well

Listen for the muted scream of Her soul
Listen for the gentle rustle of Her kiss,
When Her ecstasy triumphs
It tells you this:

"I am Mother, Maiden and all-knowing Crone,
I am the twilight path paved in stone,
I am the fiery sun emitting heat,
I am the soothing corner where lovers meet,
I am cold and snowy as winter's eyes,
I am the cobalt blue of summer skies,
I am the amber meadow of an autumn day,
I am the innocent room where children play,

I am the giver of birth and the taker of life,
I am the absolution in your moment of strife,
I am woman and man and their fusion sublime,
I am the elixir of any and every divine,
I am dawn and dusk and the in between,
I am the ruptured wound wiped new and clean,

I am the fluttery touch of a butterfly's wing,
I am the garden of seeds sprouting new in the spring,
I am the chilly sting of an intelligent stare,
I am the answer to your fervent prayer—

Whether singing in rapture or
Conceding defeat,
I am the ageless source of
An existence complete"

A Witch's Prayer for Inner Peace

May the Goddess grant me serenity and courage
To leave behind the trials of the day
And find within myself the strength to carry on,
By the power of earth and the moon
The sun and stars and the elements,
I am at peace.
I am delivered to my quietude
I am delivered to my confidence
I am delivered to power
I am delivered to my grace
I am delivered to the knowledge of sacredness around me

Conclusion

The Goddess and God are alive in nature at every turn; when one accepts this philosophy, his or her concept of divinity shifts into something intimate and personal. We draw power from that intimacy, and from that power come the seeds of magick. Americans are quickly adapting to this train of thought. They are shedding the old coat of patriarchal dynamism and looking ahead, into a future that will undoubtedly partake of New Age ideas: astrology, the paranormal, magick. Oddly enough, this means looking into the past. American history is alive with examples of shamanism and folk magick, and our multicultural tapestry has never completely excluded the Witch, midwife or medicine man. The Witch of today is more educated than ever before; he or she knows that Witchcraft is not a new fad. As we have seen with so many aspects of popular culture, anomalies do not have much of a life span in the United States. Wicca and Witchcraft, however, have been with us for a long time, and they continue to grow.

When *American Witch* discusses magick, it does so on a twofold scale. On the surface, the magick in this book is of the customary spell and ritual variety, but on a deeper level, it is about the discovery of the magickal self—this country's and your own. American Wicca is a mosaic of traditions and concepts, and therein lies the source of transformation and successful practice. The modern seeker is not only interested in casting a spell; he or she wants to know how much farther one can go with the magick—and where it leads. The American Witch wants to walk between the worlds while still living responsibly and fearlessly in this one.

One Nation Under the Goddess

The following is a state-by-state resource directory containing occult shops and other esoteric supply businesses. It is not an exhaustive list, but practitioners in all major cities and surrounding suburbs will certainly find a link or two to explore.

Wiccan/Pagan Organizations

Covenant of the Goddess
537 Jones Street, # 2887
San Francisco, California 94102
www.cog.org

Witches' League for Public
   Awareness
P.O. Box 909
Rehoboth, Massachusetts
   02769
www.celticcrow.com

Witches Against Religious
   Discrimination (W.A.R.D.)
44 Walnut Street
Great Falls, South Carolina
   29055
www.ward-hq.org

Church of All Worlds
CAW Central
960 Berry Street
Toldeo, OH 43605

New Age/Wiccan/Occult Shops

Alabama

Lodestar and Café Luna
2827 Highland Avenue
Birmingham, Alabama

Touch of Love Aromatherapy
  Shoppe
100 Co. Road
450 Lot # 6
Centre, Alabama

Shadows and Light Shoppe
401 8th Street SE
Decatur, Alabama
www.alabamawitchshoppe.com

Alaska

Aurora Dawn's Ye Ol Apothecary
  and Hermetic Shop
Edgerton Highway
Kenny Lake, Alaska

Arizona

Enchanted Forest
476 West White Mountain
Boulevard
Lakeside, Arizona
www.enchantedforestshoppe.com

Two Hawks Herbs
8227 Northwest Grand Avenue
Peoria, Arizona
www.twohawksherbs.com

Alpha Book Center
1928 E. McDowell Street
Phoenix, Arizona

Arachne's Web
15049 North 25th Place
Phoenix, Arizona
www.witchtools.com

Mary Clyde's Magickal
  Cupboard
4710 N. 16th Street
Phoenix, Arizona

Magickal Paths
7 West Baseline Road
Tempe, Arizona

Arkansas

Spirit's Landing
1020 Van Ronkle
Conway, Arkansas

Mystic Pleasures
211 N. Greenwood
Fort Smith, Arkansas

Arsenic and Old Lace/The
   Witch Shop
722 Park Avenue
Hot Springs, Arkansas

Mystical Beginnings
Route # 2
Box 222
South Highway 59
Noel, Arkansas

The Broom Closet
2204 Parkway Drive
North Little Rock, Arkansas
www.the-broom-closet.com

Mystical Encounters
1400 W. Walnut Street
Rogers, Arkansas
www.mysticalencounters.com

California

Legends of Fantasy
5670 West End Road
Arcata, California

Moonlight Herb Company
129 1st Street
Benicia, California
www.moonlightherbs.com

The Secret Cottage
7332 Gail Way
Fair Oaks, California
www.thesecretcottage.com

The Way of the Magi
39825 Paseo Padre Parkway
Freemont, California
www.wayofthemagi.com

The Witches Grove
711 Lancaster Boulevard
Lancaster, California
www.witchesgrove.com

Whispered Prayers
120 San Juan Drive
Modesto, California
www.whisperedprayers.com

Ancient Ways
4075 Telegram Avenue
Oakland, California
www.ancientways.com

The Crystal Cauldron
234-A West Second Street
Pomona, California
www.willowscrystalcauldron.com

The Rainbow Bridge
351 North Lake Boulevard
Tahoe City, California

Colorado

Celebration New Age Bookstore
2209 W. Colorado Avenue
Colorado Springs, Colorado
www.celebrationstore.com

Isis Books and Gifts
5701 E. Colfax Avenue
Denver, Colorado
www.isisbooks.com

Quantum Alchemy
913 Corona Street
Denver, Colorado
www.quantamalchemy.com

Connecticut

Gayle's Thyme Shoppe
316 Hazard Avenue
Enfield, Connecticut

Garden of Light Spiritual
    Wellness Center
50 Thomaston Road
Litchfield, Connecticut

The Magick Mirror
321 Boston Post Road
Milford, Connecticut

Mystical Horizons
Route 27 North
Old Mystic, Connecticut
www.mysticalhorizons.com

Realms of Enchantments
16 McDermott Avenue
Old Mystic, Connecticut
www.mysticalhorizons.com

Delaware

Bell, Book and Candle
115 W. Loockerman Street
Dover, Delaware

The Magickal Cat
P.O. Box 642
Rehoboth Beach, Delaware

The Dragon Queen's Lair
803 Bradywine Boulevard
Wilmington, Delaware

Florida

Mystical Boutique
1512 E. 14th Street
Cape Coral, Florida

Sacred Space
2987 Bellvue Avenue
Corner Shops 13 & 14
Daytona Beach, Florida
www.sacredspace2001.com

Merlins Vision
100 S. Woodland Boulevard
Deland, Florida
www.rowangrove.org

Moon Goddess
4018-B
N.W. 6th Street
Gainesville, Florida
www.moongoddess.com

Stone Circle Productions
10610 Devco Drive
Port Richey, Florida
www.stonecircleproducts.com

Crystal Connection
1233 Apalachee Parkway
Tallahassee, Florida

Georgia

Bio-Buzz
612 North Slappery Boulevard
Albany, Georgia
www.bio-buzz.com

The Silver Lotus
155 Powers Ferry Road
Marietta, Georgia

Hawaii

Prosperity Corner
1156 12th Avenue
Honolulu, Hawaii
www.prosperitycorner.com

Sedona
1200 Ala Moana Boulevard
Honolulu, Hawaii
www.sedona-hi.com

Idaho

Crone's Cupboard
3601 Overland Road
Boise, Idaho

Shaddow Domain
175 S. Eastern Avenue
Idaho Falls, Idaho
www.shaddowdomain.com

The Purple Moon Crystal
   Company
50 East Main Street
Lava Hot Springs, Idaho
www.purplemooncrystal.com

Illinois

Cathy's Crystal Rose
1037 Curtiss Street
Downers Grove, Illinois

Wings of Wisdom
1117 Plainfield Road
Joliet, Illinois

The Hideaway
215 N. Water Street
Wilmington, Illinois
www.hideawaystore.com

North Wind Spirit Shop
www.northwindspiritshop.com

Indiana

Spirit Tomes & Treasures
6445 Kennedy Avenue
Hammond, Indiana
www.spirit-tomes.com

Castle Brooks Spiritual
  Supply
610 Columbia Street
Lafayette, Indiana
www.spiritual-supply.com

Moonstone Abbey
52565 U.S. 33 North
South Bend, Indiana

Iowa

Free Spirit
P.O. Box 1316
Keokukia, Iowa
www.onefreespirit.com

Kansas

Gaia's Garden
213 S. 5th Street
Salina, Kansas

Enchanted Willow Alchemy
  Shoppe
418 S.W. 6th Avenue
Topeka, Kansas
www.enchantedwillow.com

Kentucky

Moonstruck
610 Baxter Avenue
Louisville, Kentucky
www.moonstruckky.com

The Faerie Realm
1727–29 Madison Avenue
Covington, Kentucky

Nature's Magic
2018 Brownsbow Road
Louisville, Kentucky

Louisiana

Stardust & Moonbeams
22083 Highway 59
Abita Springs, Louisiana

Shadow of the Shuv'hani
Baton Rouge, Louisiana

Lady Felicia's
400 Vallette Street
New Orleans, Louisiana

Maine

Leapin' Lizards
56 Maine Street
Brunswick, Maine
www.leapinlizards.biz

Winter Ravens
1 Water Street
Machias, Maine

Crystal Crescent New Age
  Treasures and Gifts
103 Congress Street
Rumford, Maine

Three Sisters Bookstore
886 Main Street
Sanford, Maine
www.threesistersbookstore.com

Maryland

Bell, Book & Candle
7684 Belair Road
Baltimore, Maryland

Waning Moon
3748 Old Columbia Pike
Ellicott City, Maryland
www.komnyers.com

The Crystal Fox
366 Main Street
Laurel, Maryland

Massachusetts

Gardenias
399 Dorchester Street
Boston, Massachusetts
www.mygardenias.com

Goddess of the Seven Sisters
8 Crafts Avenue
Northampton, Massachusetts
www.goddessofthesevensisters.com

Bones & Flowers
874 Millbury Street
Worcester, Massachusetts

Artemisia Botanicals
102 Wharf Street
Salem, Massachusetts
www.artemisiabotanicals.com

The New Moon
268 Worchester Road
Princeton, Massachusetts
www.magickisafoot.com

Michigan

Blackwoods
311 Hubbard Street
Allegan, Michigan

Crazy Wisdom
114 South Main Street
Ann Arbor, Michigan

5th Element Products
   LLC
33 N. Washington Street
Oxford, Michigan
www.5element.com

Isle of Avalon
412 E. 4th Street
Royal Oak, Michigan

Earth Spirit Emporium
P.O. Box 181088
Utica, Michigan
www.earthspirits.org

Minnesota

First Light Empowerment
Center
115 E. Clark Street
Albert Lea, Minnesota

Magus Books & Herbs
1316 S.E. 4th Street
Minneapolis, Minnesota

Present Moments
3546 Grand Avenue South
Minneapolis, Minnesota
www.presentmoments.com

Mississippi

Southern Enchantments
100 21st Street South
Columbus, Mississippi

Higher Realm
403 Suite B
West Central Avenue
Petal, Mississippi

Missouri

Ancient Wisdom
719 E. Church Street
Aurora, Missouri

Montana

Burjon's Books
2718 Third Avenue North
Billings, Montana
www.barjonsbooks.com

Nebraska

Purple Hedge Shop
2017 Central Avenue
Kearney, Nebraska

The Next Millenium
2308 North 72nd Street
Omaha, Nebraska
www.next-mill.com

Nevada

Psychic Eye Bookshops
1000 N. Green Valley Parkway
Henderson, Nevada

Wicca World
2009 Los Altos Street
Las Vegas, Nevada

New Hampshire

Pachamama
One South Main Street
Concord, New Hampshire
www.epachamama.com

Gypsy Rose's
3 Gray Avenue
Farmington, New Hampshire

Kitt's Dream
123 Hanover Street
Manchester, New Hampshire
www.KittsDream.com

New Jersey

Charmed in Company
849 West Bay Avenue
Barnegat, New Jersey

Inspirations
205 Main Street
Hackettstown, New Jersey
www.inspirationspirit.com

The Celtic Cauldron
5 West Front Street
Keyport, New Jersey

Spellbound
5 Gillen Road
Rutherford, New Jersey

New Mexico

Abitha's Herbary
3906 Central S.E.
Albuquerque, New Mexico

Moonrise Books
2617 D. Juan Tabo N.E.
Albuquerque, New Mexico

New York

The Flying Broomstick
158 Hamilton Street
Albion, New York

Magickal Realms
2937 Wilkinson Avenue
Bronx, New York

Medieval Mayhem
527 A Hawkins Avenue
Lake Ronkonkoma, New York

Sacred Space, Inc.
1490 Montauk Highway
Mastic, New York

The Awareness Shop
180 Main Street
New Paltz, New York

Morgana's Chamber
242 West 10th Street
New York, New York

The Dreaming Goddess
9 Collegeview Avenue
Poughkeepsie, New York

The Magic Box
376 Meigs Street
Rochester, New York

Realm of the Rainbow
46 Railroad Avenue
Sayville, New York

North Carolina

R's Gems & Rocks
4929 Bragg Boulevard
Fayetville, North Carolina

Wayah Witchery
565 Wayah Road
Franklin, North Carolina

Kindred Spirits
P.O. Box 255
Sandy Ridge, North Carolina
www.kindred-spirits-nc.com

Ohio

The Runes
46388 Telegraph Road
Amherst, Ohio
www.therunes.com

Midnight Muse
1981 Madison Road
Cincinnati, Ohio
www.midnight-muse.com

Fly-by-Night
2275 North High Street
Columbus, Ohio

Oklahoma

Curious Goods
2701 Sheridan Road
Lawton, Oklahoma

Oregon

Woodhart. Ways of Olde
1010 Grant Street
Eugene, Oregon

Practically Magical
872 S. Highway 395
Hermiston, Oregon

Stone Circles LLC
1304 Adams Avenue
LaGrande, Oregon

Pennsylvania

New Moon
210 West Cunningham Street
Butler, Pennsylvania

Kelly's Magical Garden
43 Essex Road
Camp Hill, Pennsylvania

Goddess Circle
148 S. Broad Street
Lititz, Pennsylvania
www.goddesscircle.com

Rhode Island

Indigo Herbals
346 Wickenden Street
Providence, Rhode Island

Herbal Magick
750 West Shore Road
Warwick, Rhode Island

South Carolina

Jumping Water
813 B Savannah Highway
Charleston, South Carolina

The Dragon's Treasure
2710 White Horse Road
Greensville, South Carolina

The Keep
127 Central Avenue
Summerville, North Carolina
www.thekeep-central.com

South Dakota

Arts Mystique
11 North 5th Street
Custer, South Dakota

Crescent Moon
626 St. Joseph Street
Rapid City, South Dakota

Tennessee

Violet Moon
521 N. Main Street
Greeneville, Tennessee

Charlotte's Mystical Web
1406 N. Highland Avenue
Jackson, Tennessee

Mother Earth Oils & Herbs
119 S. Central Street
Knoxville, Tennessee

ShopKeepers
111 E. Lytle Street
Murfreesboro, Tennessee

Texas

Wild Bohemian
2911 E. Division Street
Arlington, Texas

Ancient Hallow
2410 Calder Avenue
Beaumont, Texas

The Magick Circle
833 W. Price Road
Brownsville, Texas
www.themagickcircle.com

The Magick Cauldron
528 Westheimer Road
Houston, Texas

Mystic Heart
124 S. Main Street
Irving, Texas

Utah

Gypsy Moon
1011 East 900 South
Salt Lake City, Utah

Mystic Dragon
2132 South Highland Drive
Salt Lake City, Utah

Vermont

Upward Spiral
28 Village Square
Bellows Falls, Vermont

Circling Aquarius
96 Randall Hill Road
Springfield, Vermont

Virginia

Gargoyle Manor
3160 Dry Pond Highway
Claudville, Virginia

Village Herb Shoppe
47 E. Queens Highway
Hampton, Virginia

Washington

The Healing Tree
502 16th Street N.E.
Auburn, Washington

Pioneer Books
2074 Vista Drive
Fernadale, Washington

The Crystal Garden
100 Frederick Avenue
Port Orchard, Washington

West Virginia

Magickal Realm
173 W. Main Street
Salem, West Virginia

Wisconsin

Mico Femind
906 E. Walnut Street
Green Bay, Wisconsin
www.micofemind.com

House of Magick
1210 E. Oklahoma Avenue
Milwaukee, Wisconsin
www.houseofmagick.com

The Mystic Candle
1718 East Street
Two Rivers, Wisconsin

Wyoming

Pan's Grove
458 S. Walnut Street
Casper, Wyoming
www.pansgrove.com

Online Retailers

www.magickware.com

www.spiritdimension.com

www.witchonthego.com

www.azuregreen.com

www.newageresellers.com

www.wiccanbooks.com

www.newageshops.com

www.capricornslair.com

www.witchware.com

www.magusbooks.com

www.pagannation.com

Recommended Web Sites

NewWitch Magazine
www.newwitch.com

www.paganpride.org

www.wicca.org

www.americanwicca.org

www.wiccan.com

www.modernwiccan.com

www.wicca.com

www.pagan.com

www.outofthedark.com

www.loresinger.com

www.salemwitch.com

www.thepaganweb.com

www.wiccacenter.com

www.fabrisia.com

www.witchway.net